SHAHBAZ 77

US Forces in Iran, April 1977

—

a true story

—

Curt Sanders

SHAHBAZ 77
US Forces in Iran, April 1977

© 2018 Curt Sanders, all rights reserved.

No part of this book may be reproduced or transmitted in any form or by any means, electronic or mechanical, including photocopying, recording or by any information and storage and retrieval system without the written permission from the author, except for the inclusion of brief quotations in review.

Every effort has been made to ensure that this book is free from error or omissions. However, the Publisher, the Author, the Editor or their respective employees or agents, shall not accept responsibility for injury, loss or damage occasioned to any person acting or refraining from action as a result of material in this book whether or not such injury, loss or damage is in any way due to any negligent act or omission, breach of duty or default on the part of the Publisher, the Author, the Editor or their respective employees or agents.

Every attempt has been tried to recreate events, locales and conversations from memories and documents. In order to maintain their anonymity in some instances, names of individuals and places may have changed.

Credits:
 Printed by lulu.com
 Cover — "Blind" by Sirle Kabanen, www.postermywall.com
 Page 11 — Photo, U.S. Air Force, Lockheed C-141 Starlifter.

International Standard Book Number: 978-1-7324538-0-7

Harrisburg, Pennsylvania: self-published, 2018.

You may contact the author:
Curt Sanders
4707 Hillside Road
Harrisburg, Pennsylvania 17109-5203

Dedication

To all those in the Armed Forces, past and present, who put up with the daily indignities of military life that no one ever mentions and seldom understands.

To my family and friends for their support of without, this narrative would not be possible!

Acknowledgements

I want to thank Janelle Simmons for her patience in listening to my fears and doubts about writing this book and not go crazy. She is a source of encouragement.

I also want to thank my friend Jerry Waln for getting me interested in writing and to get moving about it. His input was invaluable.

Billions of thanks to my family for the support.

Extra billions of thanks to the individuals in this book who made a little history and changed parts of my life.

SHAHBAZ 77

Contents

Dedication 3
Acknowledgements 4
Preface 7
I. Starlifter 11
II. The Twelve and their Amigos 21
III. The Mission 35
IV. Time off 43
V. Winding Down 55
VI. Weather Changes 57
VI. The Departure 63
VII. Postscript 71
Bibliography 85
APPENDIX 87

Preface

This account is not intentionally a political tome nor polemic exercise. It is part first-person memoir, part military history, and part analysis.

It was barely two years after the war in Vietnam ended. America was reassessing itself in the world. It's military forces depressed and dejected, but still alive with opportunity. As a 21-year-old recently unemployed printer from the private sector looking for a job, I joined the United States Air Force in March of 1975 — an old man of 22 years of age compared to others with me in boot camp. After six weeks Basic Training at Lackland Air Force Base (AFB) in San Antonio, Texas and eight weeks of Technical School at Lowry AFB, Denver, Colorado, my first permanent duty station was at Royal Air Force (RAF) Lakenheath, England. Arriving in the land of green grass and gray skies on a cold, windy, dank day in July, began my two-year sojourn in England.

Twenty-one months later, April 1977, I inadvertently made history with eleven other airmen on a temporary duty mission (TDY) to Shiraz, Iran. I kept some mementos from "Exercise Shahbaz 77" buried in a scrapbook for decades feeling it was an insignificant blimp in a rather lackluster five-year military tour of duty. Upon my honorable discharge in 1980, I attended college and I wrote a paper for a course in 1983 about the experience and it was nearly published in a magazine. Rejected and dejected, I buried the account for a few more decades. Years went by and with nagging reminders from self, friends, grandchildren wondering what I did in the Air Force, and constant reminders about the Middle East in the news, retirement time finally compelled my hand to research what happened on that mis-

SHAHBAZ 77

sion. What was it all about? What was my part in the cog of the machinery? The movie *Argo* (2012) and its portrayal of that now declassified operation two years after Shahbaz 77, finally prompted me to contemplate writing this narrative.

Research into Shahbaz 77 was sparse with practically nothing found about the Exercise on the Internet or elsewhere. Even the name of the exercise had its variations: Shabbazz 77, Shabazz 77, etc. Correspondence with the Central Intelligence Agency, and Pentagon Freedom of Information offices yielded little. The US Air Force historical agencies couldn't find anything significant. Alas, a USAF Historical Research agency person, after a year of reading my frustrated emails and letters, called me on the telephone. She said such exercises were rarely archived unless they had significant historical relevance. She was kind enough to send a CD that contained only brief information about the Exercise. Bottom line: I am the archive from the "souvenirs" and personal journal notes I made at the time.

Before my memory fades further and is totally distorted with time, this is the recollection over four decades later.

Thank you for taking the time to read this.

SHAHBAZ 77

"Shahbaz" — royal falcon

*"A mountain never meets a mountain,
but a man meets a man."* —
Persian proverb

SHAHBAZ 77

I. Starlifter

The Elevator to Hell seemed to rest for an eternity after it stilled on the runway. The sudden silence of the engines was deafening — you could hear a pin drop. No one seemed clear what to do next — heck, we just landed on Mars!

Huh, I guess we're here now.

§ § §

The bucolic East Angelia Fenlands of County Suffolk is owned beauty and romanticism — and more indebted when it wasn't raining. After duty hours at RAF Lakenheath often came with a welcome retreat to the countryside from the hustle and bustle of work and military base life.

RAF Lakenheath was a USAF operated base under the permission of the Royal Air Forces of the United Kingdom.

SHAHBAZ 77

In 1977, it was home to the 48th Tactical Fighter Wing stocked with F-4 Phantom jets, ready to launch in minutes into Eastern Europe and strike a blow against the "Evil Empire." The F-4s were noise hogs and it made the base very thunderous at times.

The lush green countryside and picture postcard scenes of The Fenlands was like a drink of warm coffee in the morning. Nearby Thetford Forest was a favorite repose in solitude for reflection and reading. I had just finished reading *Akenfield — A Portrait of a Suffolk Village* by Ronald Blythe[1] given to me by Rev. Roy Rimmer, a local Church of England pastor whose church I attended when not working. *Akenfield* would later become a classic book and a basis for my own socio-political convictions. "People were being worked to death for others," Rev. Rimmer told me as he handed the gift to me. It would become applicable to other villages around the world.

My co-workers and I were serving up lunch at the base diner on an unusually pleasant April 1st in 1977, when "the boss" Don Hatcher circled around me. "Say, Airman Sanders, I know you're 'short' in a few months, but would you be interested in going TDY [Temporary Duty]? I understand it's only for a month." My two-year tour in England was soon to be up in July making me "short" in military speak. I was expecting my next orders to another base somewhere in the world soon. I hesitated to answer in part not wanting the disruption in my life and half thinking it was an April Fool's joke, but Master Sergeant Donald Hatcher wasn't the type for jokes. "Okay, think about it," he said, seeing my indecision. But before he exited the hot, steamy food table area I was working in, I turned to him

---

[1] Blythe, Ronald. *Akenfield — A Portrait of a Suffolk Village.* 1974.

SHAHBAZ 77

and shouted, "okay, I think I want to go. I want the experience and I feel I'm getting stale here. Where to?" I asked with an enthusiastic curiosity. "Can't tell you now — it's classified." Classified? Hmm... I was even more interested now, and peaked anticipated change of pace, spiced with a little apprehension. The old military proverb: "never volunteer for anything" was ringing in my head, hoping I wouldn't regret volunteering. Oh well, I signed up with the USAF not only to have employment, but also for some adventure. Okay — go for it Curt!

"Report to me tomorrow at 0800 at my office," he smiled back.

He tapped two other co-workers, Airman First Class [A1C] Derek A. Reuben and A1C Mark L. Thomas, who also volunteered. It was my chance to get to know these new fellows better. Derek and Mark had arrived only about six months before to Lakenheath but were on other shifts most of the time. Since Hatcher made it sound like a short duty, and we thought about the extra cash as well as the change of pace.

The following day we three arrived on time at "Hatcher's Hole" — an affectionate nickname for his office. He gathered us in like a mother hen, closed the door, and made sure no one was around but the four of us. Hatcher was a professional NCO and suffered no fools. Inside that tough exterior was a soft-spot for his troops — he made work more bearable and he was fair — so we respected him. He operated the Dining Hall like a dressed turkey on Thanksgiving Day: neat, tidy and good restaurant type presentation. He even had the dining hall compete with other base dining halls, scoring points on ambiance, cuisine and culinary skills. He was proud of us. Hatcher knew the up coming new food service specialists were well trained at Lowry.

SHAHBAZ 77

The Air Force was moving away from the old stereotype "mess hall." Indeed, my food service training at Lowry was often under the guidance of four-star chefs.

"What I am about to tell you is classified Secret. So, no talking to anyone about this from here in out — read me?" We nodded our heads affirmatively. We were trained in the handling of classified information and already had Secret clearances. As food service specialists, we often prepared food for classified missions and had the knowledge of troop movements. Earlier, I did a six-month stint at the base's Victor Alert center requiring a more intense background check.[2]

"The TDY is to Iran, starting April 7th. You'll pack a duffle bag with the standard work uniforms. Plus, bring civilian attire as you won't be allowed to wear uniforms off the base. They're callin' this Exercise Shahbaz 77," as he slowed and stumbled on the exotic sounding name with his southern drawl. At first, I thought he said "Shazam" — coming from the Gomer Pyle television series and starring actor Jim Nabors. *Geez, they were Marines, not Air Force - they couldn't even get that straight?* I thought. "What was that name?" we chorused altogether. Hatcher again looked closely at the set of papers in front of him, and repeated "Exercise Shahbaz 77 — I don't know what that means" and he shrugged it off and moved on to other business.

Iran? Wow! As an "A" student in geography and world history in high school, I was well aware of its location and

---

[2] Quick Reaction Alert, or more commonly known as Victor Alert. The job of bomber crews was to provide tactical nuclear weapons at a moment's notice, providing targeting options in Eastern Europe and deterring Soviet forces from concentrating conventional forces and firepower. It was a highly secure and secretive base-within-a-base where everyone slept and ate separately from the main base.

some history. I was quite electrified and started day-dreaming about it.

"You'll be housed in a regular tourist type hotel and working from an established base kitchen, so it's not a field operation."

Even better!

Mark, in his own witty way, said he was glad being billeted in a hotel, "I don't want any bugs crawling around on me" fearing an outdoor tent tour. He pontificated a few seconds too long before Hatcher, taking him too seriously, said, "Oh for God's sake Thomas, no bugs are going to bother you. Stop talking like that! You're not going to be camping out." Derek and I just snickered at Mark who realized he was being made fun of and shot us a glare.

"You'll be teaming up with other units from USAFE [United States Air Forces Europe] and *will be the first food service military unit to deploy for a rapid deployment exercise in the Middle East."* The significance of that sentence went right over my head, not sinking in, still dreaming about ancient Persia. I was trying to bring up every scrap of information I could think of about Iran from my schooling, while half listening to Hatcher's dissertation on in-country behavior and finances. When he finished, he dismissed us and reminded us to keep our mouths shut.

Later that evening, I went to the base library and discretely looked over some maps and history. I was really going to Iran — a place of deep ancient culture and history! I was still pinching myself. But I did something I wasn't supposed to do: tell another person who didn't have a need to know. My friend, A1C John Pearson, who worked in the weapon's storage area at the base, had also graduated from Lowery AFB as I did (but obviously from different schools), he understood the gravity of what I was telling him, so I felt safe to confide in him.

"Iran?" John's eyes widened. "You're going to Persia?" He hushed quietly with a hint of enigma in his voice as we sat in my barracks room. "Tell me no more — these rooms have ears."

"Oh come on John, no one else is around!" I was bursting to tell someone!

"Wow Curt, what an experience you'll have — but I can't know more," he exclaimed in his heavy New York City accent. I agreed and thanked him — I just needed to share my excitement with someone else. I wasn't close with my soon-to-be travel companions Derek and Mark. John and I didn't talk about it further until I returned in May 1977. I was allowed to tell my other buddies Stu Rothberg, Bob Slotness, Mike Pascoe and Ken Nordstrom, that I was leaving for a month — for somewhere in the world.

I went to sleep in my bunk-bed thinking, *wow! This type of opportunity doesn't happen in a lot of people's lifetimes. I don't know anyone personally who has ever been to Persia.* It was pretty much the same thinking when I welcomed my orders posting me at RAF Lakenheath. Some people wait until their retirement years and save up a fortune to visit such places. My mind flashed back a few weeks to a retired American couple in their 60s that I met on a train near Cambridge one day. They heard my American accent after speaking to a conductor and asked for help heaving their luggage. "Boy, these trains do run on time don't they? We hardly had time to change trains. Thanks for the help with the luggage," I remember the man saying to me as he huffed and puffed from exertion. His wife asked if I was a tourist also. "No ma'am, I'm stationed here with the U.S.

SHAHBAZ 77

Air Force for two years." She recoiled and said, "you're a damn lucky boy." Yes, I was feeling lucky and blessed.

Within a couple days orders were cut and we three gathered at our transportation point in the base, traveled a short distance down the road and boarded a Lockheed Starlifter C-141 at RAF Mildenhall courtesy of the 513th Tactical Airlift Wing, Military Airlift Command. After a short trip across the Channel, we landed at Ramstein AFB in Germany an hour or so later. W were bussed a short distance for incoming processing, and had supper at an Army Mess Hall. It was an okay dinner, but paled to our USAF "chow." I don't know why they took us to an Army outfit, and that evening we were billeted to Army housing. It was fine, but a tank crew was in town on TDY and they were a bit rowdy. I shared a room with a "tanker" who wasn't into the partying, and not talkative with me either.

Next morning a USAF Master Sergeant knocked on my door at 0600 and announced he was my new NCO [Non-Commissioned Officer] for the TDY and to report downstairs at 0800 after breakfast mess. I showered-up, dressed, and went downstairs in my USAF uniform to the Army dining hall and produced many stares and cat-calls. Okay... USAF diners were miles ahead of them — Army powdered, reconstituted eggs wasn't very appealing to me — I ate lightly.

Our new boss, with papers in hand, gathered us up via a base car to the airport. We boarded another Starlifter late-morning and a few hours later ended up at Incirlik Air Base, Turkey. The box lunch we had in-flight sated my appetite left wanting from the Army "breakfast".

As we disembarked, a rather attractive flight-line airman greeted us with an authoritative "welcome to Hell" with her hands on her hips, sternly glaring at us. I supposed the "Hell" was the heat. Yeah, it's hot in southern Turkey this time of year, but it was a nice change from the cold April English bleak skies with green grass fed daily by endless rain. And… she was a welcomed sight to see.

Adona, Turkey was hot, sunny and arid looking, but it had the smell and humidity of the nearby Mediterranean Sea. The airman was blonde, blue-eyed, well fit into white short sleeves and short pants which accented her great tan from working on the runway. I was surprised by her white uniform often reserved for medical and food troops like myself. The white cloth reflected the heat off the hot runway better than olive drab fatigues. And, to my disappointment, learned she wasn't going TDY with us!

It was here that we finally met up with the rest of "the Twelve" USAF food service and other personnel as they flew in from other European bases — we were the nexus group for this exercise. After a few hours waiting at the airport, we finally boarded another Starlifter for Shiraz, Iran. The seats in this C-141 were like passenger seats on a commercial airline, unlike the previous very uncomfortable "jump" seats along the side of the plane. The interior was still cold and deafeningly noisy.

As we learned in the cacophonous briefing on the plane after lift-off from Incirlik, we sojourners were going prior to a larger force who were to deploy in less than two weeks. We would be in support of 300-400 other airmen at Shiraz Air Base who would be training with the Iranian Air Force. Besides Derek, Mark and I from the 48th Combat Support Group, we had two female members from RAF Upper Heyford, five other male members from German bases, another male member from a base in England. A thirteenth passenger was a young, large and often sweaty administrative lieutenant who handled the finances and "paperwork."

I learned years later that the British Royal Air Force was to join the exercise, but canceled due to security![3] The dissident group the People's Strugglers, assassinated five Americans in May 1975, "... and further attacks are likely."[4] We had no warning about any threats except the usual "America stops three miles outside its shores" so-be-warned-and-be-alert mantra. It never occurred to my naivety that someone would actually want to kill me just because I was an American.

Our leader, Master Sergeant Douglas Chamberlain, who was posted from a base in Germany, had already been to Iran a month before, scoping out the Iranian Air Force base and making contacts. He was an affable fellow and had those leadership qualities you expect in a senior non-commissioned officer. Also, aboard the plane, we heard news of a major earthquake in Iran just north of where we were to be deployed in Isfahan Province.[5] "From what I hear, nothing to worry about," he said. We weren't too concerned about it either, but it did append to our apprehension of going into the unknown. Airmen are a superstitious lot, it added to the fabric of an unseen foreboding as a sign of things weren't going to be as smooth as we figured on our "safari paid vacation in the sun."

---

[3] Dimkrakis, Panagiotis. *Failed Alliances of the Cold War: Britain's Strategy and Ambitions in Asia and the Middle East.* New York: Tauris Academic Studies, 2011.

[4] Central Intelligence Agency. *National Intelligence Daily Cable,* April 15, 1977. Declassified and approved for release June 9, 2005; previously Top Secret; page 6.

[5] April 6-7, 1977 major earthquake, killing 167 people around the town of Bandar Abbas. It measured 7.0 on the Richter scale.

SHAHBAZ 77

The flight from Incirlik to Shiraz was uneventful. Most of us had drifted off to light sleep. The drone of the plane was hypnotizing and the crew chief had passed out blankets that added warmth to the Land of Nod.

As we neared the airport, the crew chief came out and shouted that the co-pilot was fairly new to flying and wanted to practice a "combat dive" into the base. I had no idea what that meant. "Make sure you're buckled up tight," he smirked as he disappeared into the rear of the cabin. Next thing I remember was a sudden, deep dive after a break left. We were going down very fast — almost straight down! *Jesus, this butter-bar looey is going to get us killed,* my mind screamed. I didn't want to show fear to the others, so I kept quiet and tortured the seat handles with my grip. *Oh well, if I get killed at this speed they won't find much of me, and it'll be pretty quick. At least they'll preach at my funeral "and he died in the service of his country"* — or some kind of tripe to comfort my parents' grief.

Suddenly, the plane lurched up out of the dive and leveled off. Within seconds we smoothly landed. My ears were still popping. I heard a few sighs of relief, but I didn't dare look to see who it was. I had my eyes glued to the floor.

I later learned the "combat dive" was a technique to quickly land on a runway, minimizing enemy ground fire focused on the aircraft. I also heard it was called the "Elevator to Hell." I knew I really didn't want to repeat it again — my mind imagined all kinds of things going wrong for the pilot just as he pulled-up out of the dive.

Elevator to Hell — and we just stepped out of it into what?

SHAHBAZ 77

II. The Twelve and their Amigos

The Starlifter seemed to rest for an eternity after it stilled on the runway. The sudden silence of the engines was deafening — you could hear a pin drop. Despite our stimulating plunge from the skies of southern Iran, we were all still groggy from the trip — no one seemed clear what to do next.

Huh, I guess we're here now.

I kept looking around. Okay, what's next? The crew loadmaster opened the side door after a loud pounding from outside.

The door opened, and despite being near sunset, the bright sun pierced into the semi-dark Starlifter hold. A thin Iranian airman stood just outside of the door. "Welcome to Iran," came a monotone in clear English. He had armed men with him, all looking very suspicious at us — like they never met an American before (and probably not). Thankfully, the weapons were slung over their shoulders.

"Sir, I think you should greet him." Chamberlain urged the only officer in our ranks. The lieutenant glared back at him angrily, "I'm not f___ in charge here Sarge — you are!" I was totally stunned! I never saw or heard an officer beg down from his leadership role or use that language. It was just not right with me. Two years in military service and I guess I was still naive. I guess the officer was referring to protocol — the NCO should have greeted him.

Unfortunately, I looked at Chamberlain after the exchange and he furled his brow noticing that I somehow put him on the spot because I looked at him. "Sanders — you out first," he barked. I unbuckled my seatbelt and stepped out down the short ramp onto the sandy runway berm. Being first out, I admit I had to screwed up some courage —

everyone else seemed afraid. I looked around and saw half-a-dozen armed Iranian soldiers staring at me. Now I know what if feels like to be the subject in a zoo.

As we stood around the runway, with the armed guards checking us out, a military bus arrived and we all climbed into it. An Iranian NCO spoke some English and indicated we were to be taken to the officer's mess, as guests, for dinner. The surroundings were much like any airbase in the world — but dry, dusty and hot. We were clearly in another world here. The surrounding mountains didn't seem to have any vegetation. No one spoke much. Derek and Mark were silent. We were all hungry and wondering what was going to happen next. It felt like we just landed on the Moon and were trying to talk to some aliens.

We band of Twelve were:

• Master Sergeant Doug Chamberlain. A professional, enthusiastic and a larger-than-life man, and he was the boss. He was the right man for this job.

• Staff Sergeant Marty Bishop. Out of a German base. He was professional, rumpled and worn from time. The stereotype of a crusty but likable sergeant; mustached and smallish framed.

• Staff Sergeant James Smartz. Stationed out of a German base. A large man who moved quickly about his job.

• Staff Sergeant Tony Storms. Stationed out of a German base. An okay fellow, but with a quick temper. I remember him chewing me out for small stuff, but later he was a very likable fellow.

• Staff Sergeant John Cook. Stationed out of a German base.

• A1C Mark Stevens; another good guy to have around.

SHAHBAZ 77

- Sergeant Lee Ann Yost, she was a friendly soul from RAF Upper Heyford. She fretted about leaving her husband and family, but we became close and we were both comfortable talking to each other.
- A1C Paula Potter. She was also from RAF Upper Heyford. A pretty blonde who worked hard.
- A1C Robert Ellis. A great guy who would do anything for you.
- A1C Derek A. Rubin, RAF Lakenheath. Derek was from Philadelphia. He had the air of likable Philly edge.
- A1C Curtis D. "Curt" Sanders, RAF Lakenheath. That's me! Just an ordinary guy from the eastern edge of Appalachia in south-central Pennsylvania from a white collar working-class family.
- A1C Mark L. Thomas, RAF Lakenheath. Mark was hard to get to know. He talked a lot but revealed nothing about himself — believed to be from Chicago. He always stayed positive for the most part and worked hard.

Yost, Potter, Ellis, Rubin, Thomas, Stevens and I were all green to TDY — our first time — over half of the crew. The others were experienced.

At the Iranian officer's mess, we sat down at a very nice and ornate table. The settings were impeccable — ready for the King to arrive! The main course was a lamb kabob with rice. Some of the gang didn't like the smell or eating a lamb dish (and we were all cooks?), and ate some other things I don't recall. Others were plowing into the dish like it was their first meal in days. I told the guys around me to take it easy — you know — strange country and you don't know how the food was prepared. "Just eat enough to satisfy yourself." My advice was scoffed at.

SHAHBAZ 77

A vigorous discussion ensued at the dinner table with the Admin Lieutenant. He mentioned since the meal is "free" and that our party was going to be eating from an established USAF dining hall (once we got it set up), that separate rations (or "rats") payments would be suspended for all. Without going into the details here, it meant the married members who got paid extra for living off base would lose that money. It didn't affect me since I lived in a barracks and ate at a base dining hall. Bishop raised his voice the most, so did most of the other NCOs. Yost politely recorded her concern as she was also affected. At one point Bishop threw his napkin down and walked out, "I'll starve first before giving up my separate 'rats.'" Finally, Chamberlain had a con-flab with the dissidents and all agreed to something — not sure what, as none of it pertained to me. I keep my nose out. Separate "rats" meant something to these guys — their families depended upon it.

After dinner, we were bussed to our quarters. Eh? Where was the hotel? The abode was a half-constructed barracks with no amenities other than a hole-in-the-ground "squat" type toilet typical of the region. We all learned to sit and target the hole and not miss it! But it was a place to sleep. *"You'll be housed in a regular tourist type hotel...* I remembered what Hatcher said as I tried to sleep on a rudimentary cot with a wool blanket.

Boss Chamberlain tried to make light of the situation with an already disgruntled lot of airmen. "Made in Germany," he knocked on the walls. "German construction companies made these before the politics." Politics? What politics? It seems the German construction companies were invited to build various edifices but left when the political atmosphere got hot.

Sure enough that night, just about everyone visited the squat toilet for more than the usual bodily function. I was lucky I guess, I had eaten small. Thankfully no one was grossly ill.

In the morning, before daylight, Chamberlain roused us up and urged us to shake out our boots before putting them on. "Some scorpions may have crawled in overnight. I learned that from the last time I was here." I looked around and reminded myself that the building was wide open and in a desert. Mark, who was already paranoid about bugs, freaked out by vigorously throwing his boots down on the ground. "I don't want no scorpions" he repeated. "I don't want any crawly things on me." *"Oh for God's sake Thomas, no bugs are going to bother you,"* Hatcher's admonishment rang in my ears again. This time I wasn't laughing. I dutifully shook and stomped out my boots.

It was 0600, breakfast time and we were bussed to the Iranian officer's mess hall and treated to a meal of boiled eggs, barbari bread, and black olives. Not what we Westerners were expecting to eat for breakfast, but it tasted good. I ate the hard boiled eggs feeling they were probably, well, boiled, so they would be safe to eat. The heat of the oven would have killed any bacteria for the bread, I rationalized. The black olives? Well, I debated about eating them. Hunger won and they weren't all that bad. I had no ill after effects.

My first encounter with barbari bread was hot out of the oven and it tasted great! When we eventually got our own dining hall up and running, the bread was always cooked by the Iranians. We loved the smell and taste of hot barbari in the morning — it was a welcomed pleasure, and something that was always looked forward to in the mornings.

SHAHBAZ 77

Bishop again grumbled to Chamberlain about the separate "rats" issue. Chamberlain calmed him by saying it would be resolved. Chamberlain was very much a skilled diplomat. Unfortunately later for Bishop and the rest of the dissidents, the Air Force bureaucracy won out. Separate ration payments were to be suspended. They grumbled but followed orders.

"Tomorrow is going to be our first day at our real home for the next month," Chamberlain joyfully announced. Great, and I thought we were camping out.

After breakfast, we again boarded a military bus. After a very short trip, it pulled up to a very pleasant looking hotel near the base — the Karim Khan Zand Hotel.[6] *Ahh... finally the hotel living we were promised,* I thought. Derek, Mark, Robert and I were billeted together in one tiny room — the females in another room and the rest down the hall. At least it was clean and somewhat modern! It had a regular Western type of toilet (throne) and showers! But I had packed toilet paper as a precaution. One thing I learned from traveling to other countries that television, movies and travel bureaus never mention was the real basics: safe food, potable water and a place to relieve yourself. As we unpacked I waived my roll of toilet paper in front of my roommates, "just being a Boy Scout." They chuckled and we checked the bathroom and were all amazed to find toilet paper already supplied. Maybe this won't be so bad. But four of us to this small room? Later I "complained" to the billeting NCO who arrived with all the other mission support personnel a day later. "Hey, you're just cooks, gotta look out for the real crews with the planes — they get the

---

[6] The hotel was rather plain in 1977. Its current website, http://karimkhanhotel.com/en/ displays a beautiful, first class elegance.

best" he would smugger. The officers and the enlisted aircrew members got the high class "tourist hotel". It was the same old story — cooks were on the bottom of the supposedly "team" Air Force. And they wondered why food service personnel were stereotyped as cranky.

We no sooner settled in when Chamberlain ordered us to don our cook whites uniform and get ready to move out to our new workplace for the month. After the few surprises we had already I was a little wary of what we were going to see, but still expecting to see a fully operational mess hall just waiting for us to simply step in and start working.

Yet another Iranian military bus picked us up and we arrived at the Shiraz Air Base a very short distance away.

As we pulled up outside of the nondescript building, we noticed it was in fairly good condition. We all piled in and were given the shock of our life: an antiquated mess hall facility, overgrown with moss in some places, greasy, dirty and just horrible. *"...working from an established base kitchen..."* Hatcher's voice chimed in my head. "When was this kitchen in last use Sarge?" I inquired. "From what I've been told since the Russians were here — they built it when the Iranians were friends with them." My mind quickly raced back in time trying to calculate how long ago that was. I guess he meant 1953 when Mosaddeq was the Prime Minister. *Geez, as old as I am — 24 years!* "So, why wasn't it used since then?" I inquired. "Hell if I know" Chamberlain said with a hint of annoyance in his voice. I dropped the subject.

The air was filled with obscenities from everyone else who saw the same things I was seeing. Chamberlain put his hands up, "I know, I know, not what you expected. But the oven and grill are functional, fired by natural gas. But we have some work to do starting with cleaning this place up."

SHAHBAZ 77

We muttered our anger under our breath about Chamberlain at this point. "People. I was here a month ago and this was not the place I was shown" Chamberlain defended himself. Didn't matter — it all rolled down the shit hill, this "working kitchen".

We A1Cs and Sgt. Yost were given superiors by Chamberlain. My supervisor was Storms who made it clear he didn't like my questions to Chamberlain — I guess he interpreted them as remarks of a potential troublemaker. However, I did everything he told me quickly and quietly.

Yost and all of us A1Cs were a new generation of professionally trained food service specialists from the Lowry AFB, Denver tech school. The older NCOs were from the old school — used to dealing with other cooks who were usually misfits, criminals being punished (yeah, food service was considered a punishment in the Air Force judicial system at that time), or busted down troublesome lower quality airman made cooks as an afterthought, or disgruntled drop-outs from other professions. So, they were initially hard on us — seeing us as "problems" under a now stressful situation.

Chamberlain reminded us that we had a week to get this place into shape! The main forces that we were to feed were coming soon!

So the week from hell began. Every morning at 0330 we were aroused and picked up at 0400 by an Iranian bus and dropped off at the hall. We all worked until approximately 2000 hours every day — about 16 hour days (3:30 a.m. to 8 p.m.). We were so sick of it.

For the first few days, breakfast was mostly hard-boiled eggs, olives, and barbari bread since we had no supplies ourselves. Afternoon meals were some K-rations and what we could scrounge from the Iranians. We found the one water source was potable, but it really wasn't going to be enough for all the troops we were supposed to feed and cook for. Chamberlain was working frantically behind the scenes to get what supplies we needed.

A couple days into the clean-up, we received a pallet full of beer from the 435th Military Airlift Command Element from Rhein-Main. Yes, beer. Somehow the Air Force determined we needed that more than food or other drink. The next day it was gasoline-fired field stoves (M2A). What? Gasoline-fired stoves? I knew only of them from the books in tech school. Dangerous equipment — filled with gasoline as a quick, usable fuel source in field conditions — it was also a hot and highly volatile source. Here we go again, *"field conditions."* Chamberlain explained that the propane gas grill and oven were for cooking only and that the M2A's to be set up as a serving line heat source or augmentation in food preparation.

Storms was the only one who really had knowledge about M2A's — he had been on several TDYs in the past. He stared at the devices like he was going to do business with the devil. He sat us green troops down and explained the whole process of filling, pumping air and lighting one of these queer looking devices. "If you don't prep them right its like lighting a fuse to a bomb." I already didn't like them, but they were to be a part of our important kitchen equipment for the next few weeks. We constantly monitored the temperature gauge so it never went into the red. I could see that the other NCOs shunned the M2A's — they knew they were dangerous. They emphasized constant attention for these units.

One routine blurry-eyed morning we air-pumped up the units, getting the oxygen/gasoline mix just right to ignite it. I was tired, not getting enough sleep like everyone else. A minute later I looked at a M2A and saw it was in the red! I yelled, "Red, in the red" and everyone started scurrying around, undecided to leave or stay. Finally, Storms rushed up to the unit and looked at it hard and turned to me in disgust: "It's in the green Sanders." I timidly walked over and looked — sure enough — in the green. "Sorry, guys. I could have sworn it was in the red," I said very sheepishly and expecting a blast of hot air from Storms. Instead, he half-laughed and said, "Well, I guess we all got our rush for today." Chamberlain was heard interjecting "that got us all woke up!" I was embarrassed at the moment, but really didn't feel apologetic about it — those things were dangerous. I had to eat the ribbing I got.

As days passed, we transformed the dining hall into an *ad hoc* Post Office and currency exchange post when an A1C clerk came out of the Tehran embassy and handled some admin stuff. Later that day, another sergeant arrived who was in charge of movies. So, the "chow hall" was now multi-purposed for eating, drinking booze, administrative stuff and entertainment — a center of respite for most airmen. It became "The Ranch."

We also had a refrigerator and freezer that we cleaned and had it working by the time the main supplies came in a few days before April 15 — D-Day for us — ready to serve our first breakfast.

We had no way of making that essential drink for anyone in the military: coffee. We learned in cook school how to make "Hobo" or camp coffee only once by watching on a small scale.

Smartz would heave a huge pot onto the stove grill, and pour in some water that he measured out. After bringing it to a boil, he would throw in some coffee beans and clean egg shells and continued to let it boil for a couple of minutes. Then he threw in cold water and started skimming out the coffee with a ladle into a carafe. One of us would always be assigned to do this because the process didn't produce enough coffee in one shot for 300+ souls looking for that morning cup-o-joe. We always had a carafe sitting on one of the M2As. Luckily, it turned out great!

But it all was still a far cry from the established food service facility envisioned by us and described by our orders.

The Amigos

Every morning a small group of about four enlisted Iranian air force personal greeted us. At first, they met us with hostility as they were trained not to trust anyone coming to their new post. They soon recognized who we were, and treated us like a part of their detail. Fortunately, Resa R., an older man in his mid-thirties spoke near fluent English. The "Amigos" helped some, but their duty was to guard — and I guess watch over us. The Amigos were overall very pleasant, curious, and when we could communicate, were animated about it. GIs are pretty much the same universally in the world.

The Amigos were actually billeted in tents behind the dining hall. They were not NCO's — all conscripts into the armed forces of Imperial Iran. The better dressed NCO's arrived from somewhere else on the base. One of our visiting officers asked me "who are these guys? They dress like convicts," looking at our new enlisted Iranian air force co-workers. I explained that they were draftees into the Iranian armed forces, and not treated so well either. Their gray uniforms were tattered and worn on their thin frames. The officer simply turned away, he didn't want to hear or see anymore.

SHAHBAZ 77

"Resa R.", was an experienced world traveler, in his late thirties. He was a martial arts expert who trained with Bruce Lee in his salad days (even showed me pictures proving it). He said he was at the Olympics in Mexico City, 1968, and had visited America once and loved it. But alas, because he assaulted a man who had touched a female member of his clan, he was given a choice: prison or the armed forces. He was somewhat cosmopolitan and street educated. I felt close to him in the end.

"Grasshopper" — I don't recall his real name, was a tiny, thin fellow, very young in appearance. He was popular with the gals in our unit because he was cute. When he and the others worked, he worked hard and had that aura of integrity about him. He jumped around from spot to spot working hard, hence earning his nickname.

"Angry Man" was not too angry. He didn't like all the foreigners in his country and was very fundamentalist in his religious beliefs. However, on a one-to-one basis, he was a friendly fellow.

I don't recall the other fellows very well except to see them in pictures. Most were drafted into the armed forces and not very happy being there. A few were not very smart or educated — in fact, one was an outright idiot.

The Iranian NCO's were the professionals in the armed forces. "Sgt. Hamin" was a smooth, handsome looking man, who liked Western styles. He was a hit with the ladies. He learned English from a school he went too in Europe. Obviously, he was from an upper-class family by his bearing and education and was disgruntled because he was not an officer. He was also a very likable fellow and we talked a lot. He wanted to go to America in a bad way.

"Sgt. Davood" was a likable, aloof fellow, who kept his distance from us. He hung around a lot but didn't interact that much.

"Sgt. Snorkel" — named after the Sgt. Orville Snorkel, the comic strip character, and Beetle Bailey's nemesis. This Snorkel was also overweight and a lot meaner. He used his rank to push the conscripts around and abuse them. Once, he had about half-a-dozen of his troops lined up at attention and was berating them for something. Suddenly, he punched one in the end so hard they all fell down like dominos. At first, it was funny, but it really disgusted me. I didn't think it was professional or moral. But then again, we were not in a Western military culture, so I pretty much had to ignore it.

SHAHBAZ 77

III. The Mission

April 15th was D-Day for us. Our hard work was about to pay off — we were hoping. Everything was clean. The oven and grill were working as well as the M2A's. Days before we received a truckload of supplies: meats, eggs, frozen vegetables, etc. Pretty much the standard stuff and some of it bought off the local economy. Fruits and vegetables were shipped in from somewhere in Europe. Local fresh stuff was questionable because of the way they were grown in Iran — fertilized with human feces rather than animal feces in the West. The medic warned us away from homegrown stuff — too much of a stress on sensitive Western stomachs and a dangerous potential of picking up a strange bug.

The big supply day was a great day for us — it also meant we could eat "normal" again even if it was from a can.

Sgt. Snorkel ordered his troops to unload the truck and store the dry goods in a designated spot in the main dining hall. He kicked and screamed at them and hurried them as fast as they could work. Unfortunately, that caused some precious cargo breakage. He only screamed and kicked them all the more. I gently tried to say something but was rebuffed by him. Finally, A1C Stevens had enough and tried to tell Snorkel to ease up. Of course, Snorkel didn't speak a lick of English and thought Stevens was interfering and promptly got into a shouting match with him. It was oddly funny watching Snorkel chew in Farsi and Mark in English. Finally, one of our NCOs told Resa what to say — "more slowly please — we have time — we don't want anything broken." Snorkel got the message — he had orders not to ruffle the feathers of the guest Americans. However, it was clear he resented the interference — a usurpation of his authority in the eyes of his troops. He later learned what our rank equivalents were to him. Since half of us were A1Cs — less in equivalent rank than him — he became surly with us at times. I usually ignored him or didn't cross his path, but I kept the respect for the rank which he seemed to appreciate.

After unloading, a rope was put across the goods, as they were openly stored in the dining room, and no one but us working with them directly was allowed to cross the line. Unfortunately a few days into the Exercise a drunk US airman strayed over the line looking to help himself to free food. Our diminutive "Grasshopper" was on duty and promptly shoved him away, knocked him down on the ground, and somewhere out of thin air produced a rifle with a bayonet attached to it! That message was pretty clear! That got everyone's attention! Wow! I didn't know our Amigos were armed! I asked Resa if they had weapons on site. He was evasive and more-or-less told me it was none of my business. I asked no more after that.

The mission days for us, April 15-May 3, ran together in a blur of 12-hour plus days of work and exhaustion. The stress often erupted in getting on each other's nerves and grips. I wasn't immune to this, but we got along as much as possible. During rest periods or slow times we got to know each other and had a few days off. Not always what we wanted to do or know or cared to even know!

SHAHBAZ 77

CENTO[7] is here

Exercise Shahbaz 77 planning was begun in December 1976. Its execution, however, was in doubt from the beginning. The Turkish General Staff was reluctant to agree to the suggested itinerary from U.S. forces. Eventually the matter was cleared up.[8]

"CENTO EXERCISE - SHAHBAZ '77 was organized by CENTOs combined planning staff and is designed to test the air defense readiness and capabilities of the regional countries, Iran, Pakistan, and Turkey, and provides an opportunity for the aircrews to work together."[9]

"Shahbaz 77 involved transporting personnel and equipment from [the] United Kingdom and Germany to Shiraz, Iran. Red Flag operations evaluated air defense and tactical aircraft in simulated combat environment. Successfully utilized special operations low level tactics. Participated in numerous Emergency Deployment Readiness Exercises (EDRE)."[10]

"We are here to demonstrate our commitment to CENTO. The primary reason for exercise Shahbaz '77 is to test the air defenses system of the CENTO countries. An additional feature of this exercise will provide realistic combat training for our aircrews as they will be flying dissimilar

---

[7] The Central Treaty Organization (CENTO), originally known as the Baghdad Pact or the Middle East Treaty Organization (METO), was formed in 1955 by Iran, Iraq, Pakistan, Turkey and the United Kingdom. It was dissolved in 1979.

[8] U. S. Department of State message, December 14, 1976; Confidential; declassified May 4, 2006.

[9] [NXL] United States Air Force, *Shahbaz 77: A Newsletter For USAF Personnel Deployed to Shiraz AFB Iran.* April 1977.

[10] United States Air Force. IRISNUM 1020506. Released 1985; previously Secret.

SHAHBAZ 77

air combat training against Iranian aircraft and electronic counter measure and low level missions on Iranian ranges. The flight to Shiraz tested our interoperability with our hosts as our aircraft were refueled by Iranian KC-707 tankers," wrote mission Commander Col. Thomas G. McInerney, USAF.[11]

After April 15th, the various units rolled into Exercise Shahbaz 77; it was at this time the general operations of the TDY became declassified. "This was a small-scale CENTO-sponsored, JCS-coordinated exercise conducted in Turkey and Iran from 12 April to 5 May. The controlling MAC [Military Airlift Command] Air Force was 21AF. C-141 aircraft deployed and redeployed participating forces and support equipment from Germany and the United Kingdom to Shiraz, Iran, and return. Two 62MAW [Military Airlift Wing] C-141's deployed to Incirlik, Turkey, the primary crew staging point, in support of this exercise on 15 April and 28 April."[12]

"Six F111s, from Upper Heyford and 12 F-4s from Spangdahlem arrived here..." [20th TFW (Tactical Fighter Wing) , Upper Heyford, 52nd TFW, Spangdahlem].[13]

---

[11] [NXL] United States Air Force, *Shahbaz 77: A Newsletter For USAF Personnel Deployed to Shiraz AFB Iran.* April 1977.

[12] Richards, Charlotte D., Historian. *History of the 62 Military Airlift Wing, McChord Air Force Base Washington, 1 January - 30 June 1977*; US Air Force; CD; Twenty-Second Air Force Military Airlift Command; Unclassified; page 22. [Citing Hist Rpt, Current Ops, Apr-Jun 77 (Vol II, Sup Doc II-4)]

[13] [NXL] United States Air Force, *Shahbaz 77: A Newsletter For USAF Personnel Deployed to Shiraz AFB Iran.* April 1977.

SHAHBAZ 77

"Included in the aircraft from Spangdahlem are F-4Ds of the 23rd TFS [Tactical Fighter Squadron] and F-4C 'Wild Weasels' of the 81st TFS."[14]

Refueling aircraft tankers were provided by the Strategic Air Command KD-135 and others by the Iranian Air Force utilizing KC-707's.[15]

Other USAFE units included 12 F-4s from 401st TFW, Torrejon, AB [Air Base], Spain. The US Navy was also flying missions from a Sixth Fleet Aircraft carrier.[16] The 480th Tactical Fighter Squadron, 52nd TFW under the command of Col. Richard E. Skelton.[17] And the 50th TFS.[18]

The 12-bed mobile hospital, the 50th Tactical Air Transportable Hospital commanded by Lt. Col. John P. Westra, arrived and made its rounds for anyone needing assistance.

---

[14] ibid.

[15] ibid.

[16] ibid.

[17] IRISNUM, document 1020185 Wing/Military Airlift Command Operations, (unclassified); document 01030293 United States Logistics Group (classified), US Air Force history index. Released in 1985; previously Secret; declassified.

[18] United States Air Force, IRISNUM 01020488. Released 1985; previously Secret; de-classified.

SHAHBAZ 77

The hospital was staffed with another physician, a veterinarian,[19] a nurse and an administrator.[20]

The USS John F. Kennedy (CV 67) joined the mission from April 6 to the 19th.[21] From the Kennedy, the Carrier Airborne Early Warning Squadron, VAW-125, operated April 25-28, but left for evacuation of Kagnew Station in Ethiopia on the 29th.[22]

Early in the mission, the 1st Combat Communications Squadron out of Lindsey Air Station in Germany[23] landed and provided it's services to the end. While serving on the food line, I noticed a familiar face and the uniform lapel name "Lougee". My memory flashed back to my elementary schooling at Corpus Christi, Chambersburg, Pennsylvania to a Lougee, who was a couple years younger than me. He and his other siblings rode on the same long bus ride distributing us to our various homes in Franklin County, Pennsylvania. His face looked familiar to me.

---

[19] Although disbanded in 1980, one of the main tasks of the USAF Veterinary Corps was to ensure that Airmen—especially those stationed abroad—had access to food supplies untainted by food-borne pathogens. They inadvertently served as "medics" when no other personnel were available. Officers in the Corps post-1980, were re-designated as Public Health Officers and transferred to the Biomedical Sciences Corps.

[20] [NXL] United States Air Force, *Shahbaz 77: A Newsletter For USAF Personnel Deployed to Shiraz AFB Iran.* April 1977.

[21] https://www.history.navy.mil/research/histories/ship-histories/danfs/j/john-f-kennedy-cva-67.html

[22] Eastern Med OPS: Enclosure 3, de-classified from Confidential, June 8, 1978. A fascinating account of this little known incident is memorialized by Captain T. L. Hardin, USN "The Last Seven Days of Kagnew Station, Asmara, Ethiopia"; http://www.kagnewstation.com/finaldays/lastsevendays.pdf

[23] [NXL] United States Air Force, *Shahbaz 77: A Newsletter For USAF Personnel Deployed to Shiraz AFB Iran.* April 1977.

SHAHBAZ 77

"Hey, Lougee, are you from Chambersburg, P-A?" I asked. At first, he was incredulous and scowled at me, not recognizing me at all. "You're Tom Lougee aren't you?" He defensively replied, "yeah, but who are you?" I told him who I was and from where. His face quickly grew more welcoming and turned into a bright grin, "Hey, Curt! What a coincidence. The world is truly small. Sorry, I didn't recognize you. I wasn't expecting to meet someone I knew in the past, here." That was an understatement! Two guys from the same area in Franklin County, Pennsylvania, meeting six years later in an ancient city thousands of miles away. We chit-chatted a little as I was working the line and Tom was working to get through the food line. Later he came back and invited me to come over to his unit on the other side of the AB. "We have a shortwave phone patch back to the states if you want to make a call." I thanked him but I mentally and quickly nixed the idea. I wasn't about to go walking through an Iranian AB at night looking for them — an invitation to get shot! We talked about old times a little more, updating family stuff.

Our tag-along medic, Sgt. Vickers (unfortunately I don't recall his real name and didn't record it in my journal for some odd reason) was a great guy — helpful and carried a medical bag with him at all times. Being in a strange country where the food was fertilized by human waste, it presented problems for us cooks. We had to be especially careful about food care and what we bought off the local economy — our bodily systems were acclimated to Western cuisine, which used animal waste or chemicals for fertilizer in growing crops. Vickers had long conversations with us between meals and general gabfest. Although a medic, Vickers was not inspecting the food. In the USAF that was the responsibility of the veterinarian service — they were the "medics" in charge of our health — and very qualified ones too.

Enter Capt. John Golden, veterinarian officer, who came a few days after we set up shop at the dining hall. Dr. Golden was an easy-going fellow, down-to-earth, and talkative. He was very good at his job and helped us out in keeping everything as sanitary as possible. I had long conversations with him. He remembered his time at Hershey Medical Center in my home state and all the rigorous training he went through. I queried him a lot because, the time at my next duty station, I intended to get out of food service and become a veterinarian assistant.

IV. Time off

Our food service unit was cohesive but at times the dissimilar personalities came out. I got along with most despite the stressful situation.

A1C Potter was a very attractive blond. I didn't know much about her except, at age 14, she said she snuck away from her home in New York and attended the nearby famous Woodstock Music and Art Fair, 1969. I was impressed with that. She was a good worker, but inordinate attention from other male airmen was disruptive. Certainly not her fault. As with any human being, she liked the attention. Unfortunately, the male members were bothersome. Sgt. Yost, her roommate, had to go up the chain of command to Chamberlain to complain about her nocturnal visitor.

Toward the end, Potter got into a fray with Sgt. Hamin. Hamin misinterpreted Potter's friendly overtures and it nearly became an international incident (well, at least in our small international world at The Ranch). Potter and Hamin had kept their flirtations to themselves. As we all boarded the bus one early morning, Hamin stormed up the steps following Potter. He was obviously angry and upset. She kept pushing him back, "get away," she repeated at different times. Yost, her roommate, rolled her eyes — the rest of us deduced the scenario. I tried to ignore the whole soap opera presented in front of us. Derek, Mark and I shifted in our seats uncomfortably. I heard words like "we must be married now" coming from Hamin, and "you're crazy" from Potter. Hamin became more angry and aggressive toward her — to a point us males thought he had stepped over the line. Stevens jumped in and stood between Potter and Hamin and told Hamin to, in so many words, cool off. Derek, Mark and I stood up fixing our attention on him. He got the message and retreated. I felt bad for him — no guy wants to be rejected or stared down, but it was his problem — not hers!

Back at The Ranch Hamin was fuming and glaring at us intensely. I understood his disappointment and anger to a certain degree, so I met him head-on about the situation. I simply tried to tell him that American women are very independent and have rights equal to men, or close to it. "I don't understand this... I am in love with her," he stammered. "Don't try to understand ... just try to remember it as a good time," as I tried educating him ham-handed. It didn't help at all, he went even colder with me, "You Americans... you just take..." I apologized for the incident — not as an American, but for a bad misunderstanding between genders and culture.

Potter was standing nearby listening to the whole thing. She was a bit shaken by the whole incident. When Hamin left she bounced angrily out toward me "You had no right to defend or talk about me like that." I was surprised at first. I just threw up my hands in front of her, "okay Paula — nuff said." We didn't speak to each other after that.

Yost and I got along the best I think. Lee was newly married and already missing life back in England. I never figured out why she volunteered TDY duty. She even visited me a month later at my home base when finished with the deployment. We talked like old war vets.

Derek and I got along well. Derek got sick half-way into the mission. He was up all night, and in the morning I asked him if he wanted me to report to Chamberlain that he was sick. "Yeah man, I'm not going to make it today." I asked him if he ate or drank anything suspect. By now we knew to be careful about eating or drinking "off the economy."

"Nope. Man, I get the shits just with the change of water. Even when I first came to England, the 'good' water there made me sick too," as he worked up the strength to speak. I told him that I would stay with him and Mark could tell Chamberlain where we were. Maybe we could get him med-vac'ed (Medical Evacuation) out of here. "Man, you are the best white guy I ever met, but I don't think I need med-vac'ed out — just some rest." I was surprised by what he said about the white guy stuff, and sort of snickered telling him he was just very sick.

Chamberlain later came over and ordered me to work and said he would have the medic take care of him. Later in the evening Derek bounced into the dining hall happy-go-lucky, ordered a beer and sat down with me, now off-duty. "You look really better Derek." "Yeah. I feel a helluva lot better now. Must've cleaned me out. But I don't want to go through that again! Remind me not to go TDY again except to the states," he grinned. Derek then talked of home in Philly and how he had a son and wanted to get back. Largely the *tête-à-tête* was of general stuff — it was all good. He had a great sense of humor. Both of us got mildly drunk together.

The Bazaar

Storms was cantankerous and by-the-book when it worked his way. We clashed at times and because of his rank, I had to take the gruff. However, he surprised me one day and asked if I would accompany him to the Shiraz Bazaar (marketplace) on one of our rare days off. He and Smartz hired a cab driver (I also pitched in for the cost) and we wandered around the bazaar for a few hours in our civilian clothes of course, but everyone knew we were the new foreigners in town from America. On our way to the bazaar the cab was surrounded by thousands of demonstrators and I saw some fights in the street. Our cab wasn't surrounded because of us, we were just innocently driving down the street. But the worried look of the cabbie made me realize this was not the best situation to be in. "Please get down," he said in very broken English. We slouched down and he continued to drive on. Admittedly I was scared and the images from the movie *Argo,* (2012) where the car was engulfed in angry people, brought back that memory later in life. As quickly as the mob gathered, it disbursed.

Storms had with him several of those then new-fangled hand electronic calculators that we now take for granted in dollar discount stores in the twenty-first century. He would approach a shopkeeper, indicating he wanted to buy something and would whip out the calculator in front of the merchant. Of course, the Iranians were enticed by this new technology and offered to buy it from him. I asked him if that was legal. We had been told to buy goods only in Rials — Iranian cash — no bartering or selling stuff. Storms was irritated by my rookie question. "In this part of the world you barter" he exclaimed. Later, we moved on to another merchant booth and again he whipped out another calculator. "You have another?" I naively asked. "Shut," he quickly bumped me with his elbow. Again, he sold another to a merchant. "I need to make a few extra bucks. I have a wife and kids at home." Although I realized we were technically in violation of a *policy* I soon learned Storms was right: this was a part of the world were you dickered and traded for everything — its part of the culture!

Smartz was an experienced value hunter for antiquities. He bought a lot of glittery things. I didn't have much money on me, but I did buy a handmade wooden inlay jewelry box and a tin vase — only the vase survives today. Despite civilian attire, we looked like the stereotypical tourists coming back to the hotel. Our haircuts and lack of women and children accompanying us made us a dead give-away as military members.

It was the foray into the market that, on the way back, we picked up the admin Lieutenant. I don't recall the details, except the four of us, crammed into the cab. Iranian highways were well built and maintained, but that lead to crazy and undisciplined driving! That's putting it mildly! I thought Europeans drove fast, but the Iranians get the gold star for daring driving! They didn't even pay attention to the lines on the road.

A bicyclist was on the road peddling away when another car in front of us hit him hard and he fell to the ground, splitting his skull, spilling his brains. We were all in a state of shock. I had witnessed a horrific traffic accident at age 18 in my home county — burning bodies and all, but it was still a horrific scene. Worse yet, the car driver kept on going, not even stopping. Smartz and Storms were mildly upset. When we got back to the dining hall, Bishop was kneading some ground beef in preparation for a meal. The Admin Lieutenant took one look at it "I think I want to vomit; it looks like his brains" he blurted out and rushed off to the nearby "head." To this day, I'm not really fond of looking at ground meat.

Another day-off came and looking for adventure. Resa suggested going to town to shop in the bazaar. Since no one else was off work that day, I had to go it alone. I was very paranoid — I didn't speak much Farsi despite lessons being taught to me by Resa and the other Amigos assigned to us. They appreciated me taking the time out to learn their language and some scripting, and because of it, I was able to talk to them more about their lives and the situation around them. They became increasingly friendly and sought me out as the American who cared and respected them and their culture. But I digress...

Resa wrote down on a piece of paper the address to the hotel — at least if I got lost, maybe someone could direct me back. I headed out in the late morning and walked all the way downtown to the bazaar. I had a few stares despite being in civilian clothing. I still looked like an American.

I tried to suck it all in, knowing I may never visit this part of the world ever again. Most of it was beautiful, with beautiful, friendly people. But some of it was distressing — the poverty. I noticed the contrast of huge, empty buildings, built by German and other European companies, but no one living in them. I learned Iranians were forbidden to live in them. It was all apparently a money making scheme for the Western companies to build and get paid by Imperial Iran. My little talks with the Iranians revealed their disgust for this scheme — they weren't even hired to work on these edifices! The "Westerners" were the ones that were hired and paid to work. Iranians were okay with some "Westernization" and the modernization, but wanted to be treated fairly — including employment in their own country!

Walking in the bazaar I was often asked if I had spare jeans with me. I was offered as much as $45 US for a pair — a lot of money for them. The Iranian NCOs assigned to us at the base often tried to coax us into selling our jeans — a big status symbol for them. Alas, I only had my one pair — which I needed!

Also walking to and from the bazaar, a few small children constantly pestered me for food, pointing to their mouths. They were skinny and even blocked my way at times. I had to push some of them away. I didn't want to give any money or food to them, as I would be really swarmed with a mob of children. It was the hardest thing I ever did in my life — push a hungry child away — the faces still haunt me today.

$50 to Persepolis

I had another opportunity to do what I wanted one day. Our administrative airman was able to forward money to us from the USAF pay folks and exchange them for Rials at our dining hall — The Ranch. Resa suggested I visit Persepolis just north of Shiraz. He reminded me of the history of the ancient Babylon city. Earlier, I was given a choice: ride a camel or go to Persepolis. I choose Persepolis because it was part of human history and a once-in-a-lifetime opportunity. Riding a camel? Well, that would have been nice to say I did it, but to me, a lover of history, not worth much to me.

Resa said Sgt. Davood was looking to earn some extra money and was willing to be a driver and tour guide. Davood was an aloof fellow who spoke some English. After I spoke to him, with Resa's help, we agreed on a price: $50 US to take me to Persepolis. So, one morning I arrived at the dining hall and he was ready to go. He had his own vehicle, but we had to make a stop somewhere downtown Shiraz to repair a tire that took a long hour. I sure did get the stares sitting in his car while he took care of business.

We arrived at Persepolis about 90 minutes later and I did the tourist thing. Davood stood back, not wanting pictures of himself taken, but was very willing to take pictures of me. I marveled at the ancient culture and structures! The Babylonians sure believed in going big! Oddly enough, the thing that really impressed me the most was the graffiti —

some of it from the 17th century from various travelers, mostly European. I was thrilled nevertheless, with the whole visit — probably my most memorable visit in my life anywhere, aside from living in the museum called England for two years. Best fifty dollars ever well spent.

The Coca-Cola Caper

Toward the end of the mission, we were given another day off from work (April 28). This time, all three of us from RAF Lakenheath were given the day off together. Mark and Derek had no idea what to do. I really didn't either, but I pointed out the barren hills around the area and suggested we go exploring what is now Bamou National Park — and now more confident of our alien surroundings. Mark and Derek agreed it was something to do instead of watching movies at the dining hall. Today's movie was "Serpico" — we saw it before. Drinking beer all day was also getting tiresome.

We decided to walk several miles in the mild, dry heat to a hill that overlooked the Shiraz Air Base. How we never got picked up by the Iranian secret police, the SAVAK, for suspicious activity, befuddles me today. It was common knowledge they watched us all the time at the base. Anyway, we weren't too smart. From a security point, the whole idea was hare-brained. We could be arrested for being in the wrong place, but we were guys in our twenties and reckless. We were well aware of the Shah's reputation in the world toward civil liberties, and we were specifically told not to say anything derogatory about the Shah and his government. If we did, at best we would be shipped home and court-martialed or at worst, end up in some dark hole in Tehran never to be heard of again. In 1976, Amnesty International had Iran at the head of the human rights violation class in the Middle East,[24] but we were oblivious to our own safety.

We didn't bring canteens or anything with us. I only had a tiny camera. I took pictures, but the constant cloud of brown dust typical of the area obscured the view and went up our noses instead. This was pretty much how it was in southern Iran: dusty and a brown haze always present.

Finally, we realized we were dying of thirst. So, we climbed down and came to a little village outside of Shiraz and came across a vendor selling Coke-a-Cola. Mark and Derek convinced me it was safe to drink from the bottles — they were sealed and probably processed by a local authorized plant. I wasn't so sure. Earlier, visiting the Bazaar, I watched a boot-leg soda vendor clean out the bottles in the street sewer, pour the cola syrup in the bottle and seal it with a cap with a tap from a hammer!

We downed several bottles each. The merchant, and a small crowd laughing among themselves, gathered to see the amazing Americans pour one drink after another. The merchant became rattled after awhile. We couldn't understand him, but a local finally stepped forward who spoke some English and said we were buying out his entire stock and everyone was laughing at us because we were drinking so much. It was a rather comical scene. I thanked the merchant and gave him a few dollars extra for his trouble — he became much happier and his gestures welcomed us back anytime in the future. Then he surprised me, took a step forward, and said in halting English: "You must like Coke" and grinned ear-to-ear as he reached out and shook my hand. I assured him his was especially good!

---

[24] *Amnesty International Report 1 June 1975-31 May 1976.* London: Amnesty International Publications, 1976.

We returned to base to check our mail (we never received any), had a beer, and then back to the hotel to sack out.

That evening, we hung out at The Ranch — it was the watering hole for everyone. I went to the restroom and was doing my business on an ordinary Western style toilet (throne) when an airman rushed in and started using the squat toilet, but quickly begged me to let him use the lone throne at dining hall instead of the squats. He had the squirts bad — a lot of the newer TDY troops were sick. It was more comfortable defecating on a throne than guiding yourself over a hole you can't really see. Hearing the cry of how sick he was, I agreed and we quickly switched places as there was no privacy barriers between us. His groans and that of others were by now common to my ears. "Thanks, buddy, I got it really bad." Such odd things happen in unfamiliar places.

Goat Ice Cream

After finishing my business, I returned to the dining hall and Resa and the Amigos had a surprise for me: ice cream! I was one of the very few to receive this rare gift from them. They had pooled what little money they had between themselves and had bought some as a treat. After my first bite, I asked Resa why it was so sweet. "It's goats' milk ice cream made by a local farmer," he said. Then a terrifying thought overcame me: *was it pasteurized? Was it safe for me to eat?* So far, I had escaped the severe diarrhea everyone else had. My reaction was to refuse eating anymore, but I knew any rejection would be taken as an insult in this culture, so I consumed the whole thing. I had to admit, it was way too sweet for me — I still can taste that pungent sickly sweetness today!

SHAHBAZ 77

Well, within a few hours I paid for the ice cream: I was deathly sick and spent most of my time on the throne at the hotel. Chamberlain excused me for the day and the medic consulted with me — not much he could do. When I got back to England, I realized I lost 15 pounds — pushing my then five foot, nine inch tall, 160 pound body down to 145 pounds! Derek had noticeably lost weight also. Eventually, when I visited the base clinic in England, they documented it all as "enteritis" with a "sore on upper lip" but nothing became of any treatment. I eventually recovered and regained weight.

Chamberlain was sympathetic to me — he had his time of illness also and lost a lot of weight — he was a husky looking man going into the mission, but now thinned out. He had been invited to a wild boar hunt by some Iranian NCOs. A hunting man himself, Chamberlain he went along. Unfortunately, it was an overnight camp-out and they ate the pig they killed. Apparently, it wasn't cooked well enough and he got violently sick and was off two days. There was even talk of him getting med-vac'ed out. When he showed up finally for work, he was not the bubbly leader we had — drained and thin.

Boom, boom

We were coming to the last days of the mission. The Ranch was thinning out as the wing crews returned to their home bases and we had some relief from the grind of 15-hour days.

Movies like "Willie Dynamite"[25] (April 29), "Pick Up On 101"[26] (30th), "Terror in the Wax Museum"[27] (May 1).

---

[25] https://www.imdb.com/title/tt0072409/

[26] https://www.imdb.com/title/tt0069084/?ref_=fn_al_tt_1

[27] https://www.imdb.com/title/tt0070783/?ref_=fn_al_tt_1

SHAHBAZ 77

All very 'B' type quality movies, most uninteresting, were playing at The Ranch. For our Amigos, the movies were very welcomed. A few had never seen movies except the military training kind. The more sophisticated Resa complained we didn't have any action type movies. "You know, I like boom boom" he would animate to us. He said the others couldn't understand the movies very well because of the language, but they understood action! Guys are the same everywhere in the world!

V. Winding Down

The Accident

About two-thirds into the exercise I had my accident in the kitchen. The oven and grill were fed by gas-lines that were not covered over on the floor. We were constantly tripping over them. Well, you can guess what happened next. One blurry-eyed morning I was working and tripped on a pipe. I had nothing to grab hold of except the hot grill, otherwise, I would have cracked open my head. I held onto the grill, burning into my left hand as I tried to right myself up. Bishop came over immediately and was swearing up a storm about the conditions we had to work under. He looked at the peeling hand and said I needed medical attention immediately. Chamberlain was nearby and came over and looked at it then summoned for Sgt. Vickers.

Vickers wrapped my hand with an ointment and the best gauze he had and suggested I go back to the hotel if Chamberlain approved (which he did). I was in agony. It was still early in the morning, the sun was still coming up and Vickers and I were standing in front of the dining hall waiting for the now established shuttle buses going to the hotels. As we stood there in the quiet dawn, a group of six wild dogs gathered up in a line across from us, about 50 feet away. They snarled and growled at us, threatening to charge. We really got worried! Just in time, the bus came and the dogs scattered. I learned later, as Vickers was returning to the dining hall, he encountered the wild dogs again. Since nobody was with him, the dogs ran toward him, snarling and barking. He threw his medic bag at them and ran into The Ranch. They stopped their pursuit long enough to investigate his medical bag. After a few minutes, they lost interest and disappeared into thin air it seemed. Later, some of the Amigos accompanied Vickers and retrieved the bag.

SHAHBAZ 77

The next day, I ignored the pain and returned to work. My palm was healing quickly with Vickers and Capt. Golden taking looks at it daily. I tried to ignore the wound altogether. Being a guy I didn't want to show pain, worse yet, didn't want to appear as a slacker — I wanted to continue to carry my weight on the job.

SHAHBAZ 77

VI. Weather Changes

*"You don't need a weatherman
To know which way the wind blows"* — Bob Dylan

Political agitation was increasing in Iran. You could see and feel it in the air. I understood, clearly, that talking about politics with the Amigos was pretty much forbidden and dangerous and most feigned ignorance or disinterest. But a few Iranian airmen eventually trusted me enough to talk about their world. To my knowledge I was the only airman making an effort to learn their language (and script) — they appreciated that immensely! I had learned that they were very disgruntled with their government and others. Some of it I dismissed as the usual belly-aching soldiers have with authority, however, I realized it was serious. One Amigo exclaimed getting rid of the NCOs and officers and letting the grunts take over (via "fragging"). Most expressed anger over the political oppression, but not so much over the "westernization" commented about in the Western popular news media.

I found the average Iranian airman that I worked alongside with really didn't care too much about religion. The interest in religion was only in context to the overall culture that came with any conservative society: the respect of long-held traditional values. My interaction with the Amigos showed they were all enthusiastic about western goods like jeans and clothing styles. I received a distinct impression, as a society, they wanted to have western goods, but conservative values. They wanted Western stuff, but not necessarily all the mores. It was hard for me, as a young, naive Westerner to distill that out from each other.

On my days off, I saw signs of this discordance. Some men and women were dressed in what I call "Arab" attire.

A lot of the people my age and younger were very Western in appearance. About fifty percent of the women were wearing the traditional Chador; the other half attired in very conservative Western clothing. I often could not distinguish them from European tourists or Americans when dressed in Western garb. As mentioned before, I would be often stopped about my jeans and clothing — asked if I would sell my clothing to them (which I could not). Those who stopped me in the streets were often European educated Iranians and wanted Iran lightly pushed into the world of Western materialism. Later, the popular press would call these folks the supporters of the Shah because of his White Revolution to Westernize Iran. From my interactions and observations, this was totally untrue. I saw factions emerging from the coming conflict: those who wanted Western political values, those who want a little bit of both worlds and those who really had nothing to do with the West. The anti-West faction was represented in one of our Amigos, "Angry Man." But even he liked the Western goods, just not all the other "stuff" associated with the West, incorporated to mean "America." Even he was not personally hostile to Americans who were polite and realized we were visitors in his country. Unfortunately, the Ugly American still existed then. Some of our airmen were insensitive and uncaring about the "foreign" people around them. They had the "I'm an American, and we are superior" chip on their shoulders, which always made me cringe, even while living in Europe. It wasn't patriotism for your country, it was just bad manners.

The Party

One day, after a long full shift at The Ranch, Chamberlain asked Stevens and me to come with him to a little soirée that an "in-country American official" was throwing at a local hotel. I honestly wasn't really into going anywhere after a long day on my feet. A day before, Mission Commander Col. McInerney had visited our work-place and urged us to continue presenting a good face of America by mingling with our Iranian allies. In that context, despite my natural shyness, I agreed to go along with Chamberlain, not sure if I was being asked or ordered to go.

We arrived via taxi at another hotel and was greeted by an American and an aged Iranian officer who were having drinks. Besides us three, I recall only about 3-4 other people being there. I was offered the same scotch-on-the-rocks, but I declined. I was introduced to the Iranian officer and the American, but I don't recall their names. I was pretty much disinterested and tired and went through polite motions. Although not illegal at that time in Iran, I was slightly surprised to see the Iranian drinking hard liquor as it was frowned upon.

There was a lot of discussion about American-Iranian relations. A lot of niceties were exchanged. Tired, a lowly airman and a guest, I didn't speak. I wanted to be like the inconspicuous window drapes or a fly-on-the-wall.

The discussion turned to politics and the American and Iranian extolled the virtues of the progressive Shah and America's stalwart support of the Shah and his people *ad nauseam.* After some further bantering, the Iranian officer and his assistant excused themselves, saying he had an early inspection to go to in the morning.

After the Iranian party left, the patrician-bearing American settled in with some visible ease and comfort, now that he was among "his people."

"Tell me, fellows, how is it working closely as you do with the Iranian draftees?" he asked. Stevens and Chamberlain gave very neutral answers. I said nothing at first. I just was there, like a body watching a movie. The American then searched the room and looked at me directly, "what do you think airman?" Okay, despite being in civilian clothes, he addressed me militarily. I squirmed in my seat a bit thinking of a correct answer like Stevens and Chamberlain. But my mind wouldn't let it go — I guess I was still a naive person. "Well sir, I think they are going to kill their NCOs and officers and a revolution is coming soon." At first, everyone was stunned. Quickly the room erupted in nervous scoffing and groans. "Airman Sanders reads a lot," snickered Chamberlain and looked sarcastically at the American.

I realized then I should have never said anything except some dumb servile yes-man answer. Not only was I being made fun of, I possibly put my Iranian co-workers in jeopardy. Apparently, the American official was good at reading a person's discomfort, "Don't worry, nothing goes past this room" as he looked around the room in an intimidating way acknowledging the nods from the others.

Who was this guy? I kept asking myself. Finally, it dawned on me that he might be the "in-party" intelligence official or "spook" as we called them then. He pressed for more answers on the mood of the citizenry we had been in contact with. I gave honest but more conservative answers this time. I explained to him that the soldiers were appreciative of Western "stuff," but were not happy about the forced cultural changes from the Shah. He nodded but didn't seem convinced. "The Shah and his military are very much in control. No chance of insurrection and the like," as he confidently sipped his drink.

"Well, it's getting late, and you boys have to get up early from what I understand," as he concluded the party around 2300 hours. He then proceeded to wax again about how the Shah and the officers were in firm control of the country, looking directly at me. "What you are hearing is belly-aching from grunts — you'll find that in any conscripted armed forces anywhere in the world." *Maybe so, but my words turned out prophetic in the end.*

On the ride back I expected to get roundly pummeled by Chamberlain for saying what I did. The American was looking for affirmation — a yes man answer — not an honest answer from a naive, low-ranking airman. "Yes men" advance careers in the military — it had to be that way if you wanted to get ahead.

I expected to get my head knocked off as we piled into the taxi, but surprisingly Chamberlain agreed with me. "Just watch what you say in the future Curt," he enlightened. My assessment was dismissed by this alleged intel guy and his words have haunted me ever since. My anger grew slowly about it over the years. I wrote a letter to my sister-in-law when I got back to England about the tale. Later, I wrote a paper in college and nearly had it published. Unfortunately, both narratives are long gone.

I often wondered if this American fellow was one of those who wrote the infamous CIA report stating "Iran is not in a revolutionary or even 'prerevolutionary' situation" only weeks after we left Iran.[28]

For a few days after the party, I watched to see if there were any changes among the Amigos. I was worried my indiscretion would get them into trouble. Fortunately, I saw no changes — life went on at The Ranch.

Yes, I had talked to the Amigos, discreetly about their home political situation. I, personally, just wanted to learn more about them and their country as much as possible. I was aware, of the dangers of such discussions. They were draftees from farms and rural areas and felt helpless about

---

[28] US House of Representatives, Subcommittee on Evaluation, Permanent Select Committee on Intelligence, Staff Report. *Iran: Evaluation of U.S. Intelligence Performance Prior to November 1978* (Washington DC: GPO, 1979); page 5.

any change or didn't care. Resa and Hamin did speak up a little to me. Resa, in his thirties, was too old for military life and wanted to immigrate out of Iran. He saw no future. He wanted to go to Canada rather than the USA because he had visited British Columbia and loved it. I believe Resa was looking for a reasonably peaceful, neutral place to live in the world and be left alone.

Hamin wanted a constitutional monarchy and closer ties to Europe. He wasn't enamored by the Shah. Reading the history of Iran later in life, I understood why. The various ruling Shahs were never good for anyone except themselves. Hamin liked Western goods and some cherry-picked cultural items, but he was an Iranian nationalist all the way. He didn't like being lumped in as "Arabs." Iran's only commonality with the rest of the Middle East was the religion. They saw themselves as above the rest in Middle East in history, culture, and sophistication.

"Angry Man" represented the emerging political spectrum as I saw it. He simply wanted his religious (Islamic) values to run the show. He wasn't overzealous but was clearly upset with foreigners in his country who didn't show proper respect. He wanted the technology and wealth that the West was experiencing.

My biggest surprise, when the Revolution was *fait accompli* in 1979, was the emergence of the religious leaders as the heads of government. Most Iranians I met were rather non-religious types, even "Angry Man" had some room for different circumstances.

In our Dining Hall, some of the assigned and visiting Iranian personnel dined with us. When we pointed out the meat slices they pointed too was ham, an assumedly forbidden meat among Islamic Iranians, most just shrugged off and insisted on a serving. So, the religious "angle" was blown-up out of proportion, in my opinion.

VI. The Departure

Already the shuttle bus had changed its pickup/delivery times at our hotel posted on a sheet of paper in the lobby. I remember when the paper disappeared. I asked the hotel manager where the schedule was and he just looked incredulously at me and said there never was such a schedule — ever. I knew then it was a security thing. It reminded me of the reality that we may be targets. In the last few days, we had to wait and wait for the bus to come. Our Amigos said it was because some of the Iranian airmen were deserting and they couldn't get anyone so early in the morning to transport us. That meant late breakfast for the flight crews who didn't understand at all.

Once, while waiting for the bus in the afternoon, a car full of "Arab attired" men rolled up fast to us. All I could envision was a hand grenade coming at me or a barrel of an AK-47 sticking out the window. We had been briefed to be cautious about such a situation because terrorists were looking to embarrass the Shah with an incident. I looked around me for a place to ditch if something happened. I felt pretty helpless as we were totally unarmed for this deployment. Alas, nothing occurred. In this particular scenario these men were from the Saudi Arabian football (soccer) team on tour to Iran, playing in the FIFA World Cup, April 22, at the Hafezieh Stadium in Shiraz. Whew!

May 3rd. After working the morning shift, word came down to us that if anyone wanted to leave early, before the May 6 end-of-mission date, they needed to pack their bags *immediately*! May 6 was the day we were all to pack up to leave Shiraz. We had begun some packing up of unused equipment. It was decided to leave what little food we had left, behind. The Iranians came by with trucks to pick up some of the equipment. Things were getting politically agitated in Iran and we were feeling the heat from it. Plus, the exercise was winding down and staffing was not that demanding. A quick meeting was held at the Ranch. "How many of us can leave?" I asked Chamberlain. "You airmen from Lakenheath can all go if you want." Mark, Derek and I looked at each other and all concurred to leave together. My compadres and I had enough of TDY and wanted to get back to a "real" world. I had lost weight, was half sick, had a burned hand, and was tired of the stress.

At the end of an impromptu meeting, our admin officer quickly shoved travel papers into our hands. Chamberlain then gruffly barked "you have 30 minutes to get out!" Ellis, who had decided to stay as long as he could, volunteered to help stuff our duffle bags. Ellis already had his iron turned on, ironing out his uniform and grabbed our drab "fatigues" and spotted up the shirts. They were wrinkled, left in the bags as we never used them. It was a madhouse of grabbing everything you accumulate after living in a place for nearly a month!

We did have some time to say goodbye as we arrived at the Ranch to be picked up by the bus. I hugged Lee and said goodbye to a couple of the NCO's, who didn't seem to care much. Resa, in the culture of his country, came up to me and kissed me on the cheek. I was moved by this act, which meant a lot in that culture. It was acknowledging a brother-like relationship. We didn't dare exchange mailing addresses because, for him, if the political climate changed, it might mean collaboration with the Americans.

SHAHBAZ 77

We all kinda knew our history-making situation and managed to have one of the Amigos take our picture before we left. Only Potter and Storms missed out on the impromptu photo op. We were all ready to go home!

Lastly, the bus came and we were transported to the flight-line. Loadmasters were waiting for us and threw our duffle bags onto the Starlifter. We climbed in and realized this was going to be a no-frills trip back! A jeep was parked in front of our rack seats leaving no leg room. So, we propped our legs up on the jeep most of the way back to the non-stop flight to RAF Mildenhall. Needless to say, we were all very stiff when we finally debarked.

Arriving back "home."

It was England in the early morning — the cool forty-ish degrees of gray skies, with the smell of aircraft fumes and damp air. We were "home" now. After disembarking we looked for a shuttle bus to RAF Lakenheath and found one staffed by a bored, disinterested airman. As we traveled the short few miles, I looked around at the startling contrast from hence we just came. England was always green and lush. Moisture was always in the air — but at least today it wasn't raining for the short jaunt back. A quaint thatched house that I always passed many times on the road between Mildenhall and Lakenheath, had its red and white roses in full bloom and looking gorgeous. The English: they were always proud of their roses.

The bus dropped us off at the barracks area and we hopped off and agreed to meet up at the dining hall for lunch — we were starved. Our experience had bonded us together. We were laughing and telling jokes and tales already.

Arriving at the base dining hall for lunch, we first went back to the kitchen area to let our supervisors know we were back on base and finished with TDY. They were happy to see us and so were our co-workers. "Nice tan and lookin' thin Curt," my co-worker Sergeant Shelia Barton remarked with some envy in her voice. I smiled back, "Yep, I guess I got some sun." Back in Iran, at the dining hall, I was indoors a lot, but when I could I would be outside. Our hotel did have some lounge chairs in the back lot. I usually read a mini-size New Testament Bible while soaking up the sun. Occasionally other foreign folks would also be there and we would engage in small conversation if they spoke English. But the hotel didn't have many visitors — things were getting hot politically so they stayed away. I did meet one American couple with two small children in tow. However, I didn't like them — they treated the Iranians like dirt and had condescending attitudes — it was the Ugly American again. I stayed polite with them and avoided the family the rest of the time.

After lunch, Derek, Mark and I were told to take the day off and finish up any post-TDY business that we had: laundry, mail, and going to the base admin office to complete our travel forms for reimbursement. I stopped in to see John Pearson, who was looking after my 1967 Sunbeam Arrow (Hillman Hunter) automobile, to get my keys. I had lent the car to him while I was gone. John, as were the other guys, was glad to see me back in one piece. I sat down and told him my story. He persuaded me to see a doctor.

Derek, Mark and I entered the pay admin offices and talked to an airman about filling out reimbursement travel vouchers for payment. He was not too interested in what we went through and tried to cut corners with our pay. Derek was the first to become incensed. "Man, we went through Hell." Mark and I lead the charge from behind —

we wanted our due! The by-now flustered clerk told us he would do what he could and dismissed us. Derek was still spitting frustration as we left. Mark and I weren't satisfied with the clerk's answers either.

We returned to our barracks rooms to chill out, only to be summoned by Hatcher to his office. All three of us met up together and entered Hatcher's Hole. He wanted a debrief of our TDY.

A torrent of horror stories streamed out of our mouths to a point he felt like he was being jumped on. We realized he was not to blame and was shocked himself about the conditions not what he was lead to believe. I backed up and then took a deep breath and more calmly stated the facts: hotel, yes—fair, but crowded; dining hall, not so okay, dismal. Injuries and illnesses plagued us.

Hatcher raised up and took a breath and apologized for the conditions while simultaneously taking an irate phone call from the boss of the pay airman we just visited. Hatcher's demeanor changed and he fumed as he apologized on the phone and hung-up.

"Don't ever do that again. You come to me, your chain of command, with any bitches. What the heck was the idea of jumping all over that pay clerk? That got you nowhere," his voice and body raised and menaced us. We tried to explain, but he said he would try to smooth things out for us, but he was agitated. "Dismissed." Okay, I felt like an idiot. Probably won't see that extra pay now!

Nothing much was heard about our TDY "adventure" thereafter. Mark seemed to be okay other than some weight loss. Derek and I made appointments with the base clinic. I had lost weight and felt frail. My hand had surprisingly healed by now to allow me to fully work, handling food. Heck, I was still a young 24-year old healthy guy and mentally banished my ailments for the large part. I was looking forward to going home to Mercersburg, Pennsylvania for a visit in July and then onto my next permanent duty station, Malmstrom AFB in Montana. I had received my new traveling papers shortly after getting back.

We did get fair pay reimbursement after all, and I departed RAF Lakenheath for the "real world." I knew I had arrived in Philadelphia: it was a typical hot, steamy July day in Pennsylvania. It all seemed sort of strange to me. After a month in Iran, two years in England, I had to rewire my brain for driving on the right-side of the road and acclimate to tropical feeling weather. The bus was full of GI's of various branches, coming from the European theatre. As hot and muggy as it was, I felt I was home again. Amazingly, someone started singing "America" and the 40-50 of us started singing together! It was surreal.

§ § §

All-in-all, about 345 souls participated in Exercise Shahbaz 77.[29] We fed them all and earned us letters of appreciation from the mission commander and others. The troops often remarked that the "chow" was better than their home base diners and we received a lot of pats-on-the-back.

Was the Mission a "rapid deployment" force (RDF) new to the US military paradigm? Or, just a training mission as stated by Col. McInerney? The new President Carter had asked to set up a rapid deployment force in 1977. Despite reported inertia in this direction,[30] Shahbaz

---

[29] McInerney, Col. Thomas G., Shahbaz 77 Mission Commander. Letter of Appreciation, circa June 1977.

[30] Mann, James. *Rise of the Vulcans: The History of Bush's War Cabinet*. Penguin Book, 2004.

SHAHBAZ 77

77 was the first test. Although on paper it did not clearly describe the purpose of the mission, the talk among the ranks concurred it was a rapid deployment exercise. Indeed, Hatcher, in the pre-travel briefing, called it such. Shahbaz 77 was the inconsequential first test under the guise of a "training" and an intra-compatibility mission with the Iranians. President Carter signed Presidential Directive 18, August 24, 1977, establishing an RDF — a mere three months after Shahbaz 77's successful deployment. By September 1977, US Secretary of Defense Harold Brown described such organization to the National Security Industrial Association, but the "…speech was duly recorded…, but largely ignored by the mass media."[31]

So, what was the purpose of Shahbaz 77? Probably multi-purposed: military-based training and interoperability with the Iran forces. In hindsight, probably also to have a *force mècanisèe* to help the flight of capital out of Iran, already begun in 1975,[32] and possible evacuation of personnel of Western companies operating in Iran (who looked like they had long left already).

It was in 1979 when the Rapid Deployment Joint Task Force was formally birthed, but not fully funded or operational until 1980. Interestingly, the new RDF also stipulated no diverting of forces from NATO, unlike our USAFE components in Shahbaz 77.[33]

---

[31] Cooper, Andrew Scott. *The Fall of Heaven: The Pahlavis and the Final Days of Imperial Iran*. New York: Henry Hold and Company, 2016, page 268.

[32] *Amnesty International Report 1 June 1975-31 May 1976*. London: Amnesty International Publications, 1976.

[33] Isenberg, David. *Cato Institute Policy Analyst No. 44: The Rapid Deployment Force: The Few, The Futile, the Expendable*. Cato Institute, 1984.

VII. Postscript

World War II was the beginning of modern Iran for the purposes of this narrative. If one wants to dive into its more ancient history, there are plenty of resources to fetch. This author will allow you to do that on your own with the already copious amount of books written on the subject. However, a little context is needed...

We have heard much that the Middle East is all about oil. Iran is no different.

One of the reasons for writing this narrative was to make sense of this small exercise called Shahbaz 77 at a crucial time in Iran. There had been prior Shahbaz 75 and 76 exercises, but little is known of them. It is assumed they were also small exercise junkets to Iran. A Shahbaz 78 apparently was executed in Pakistan in April 1978, however, it was not related to Iran.[34]

Prior US military involvement in the Middle East was limited in physical appearance, but evident in the 1973 Yom Kippur War support of Israel and succeeding oil embargo by Arab OPEC nations. The Arab oil embargo ended in March 1974 after the 1973-74 stock market recession, and it followed going into 1975. Subsequent widespread unemployment in the US, going by the conversations with others in "boot camp" with me in March 1975 at Lackland, was the reason many fellow airmen ended up joining the USAF. The President, Richard M. Nixon, imposed the hated gas rationing plan, wage freezes, road speed reductions and more were implemented, leading to long, angry car lines at fuel pump stations and violent trucking industry

---

[34] Hussain, Jamal. *Joint USAF / PAF Air Exercises in 1978.* https://defence.pk/pdf/threads/pafs-exercises-from-around-the-world.124858/

clashes over diesel fuel. These impositions were later moderated by President Gerald Ford.

Because of the oil-induced recession of 1973-1975, the US looked to leadership in the newly elected President Jimmy Carter, January 1977. The oil companies were looking for a way to cow the oil-producing actors into not doing something like that again. Plans began afoot to subordinate OPEC nations into the will of US oil policies.

It was evident in April 1977 that Iran's economy was in trouble. The "Amigos" were openly upset with the rising inflation from the influx of foreign currencies exacerbating the situation. The *conscripted* armed forces of Imperial Iran were poorly equipped, clothed and provisioned from the author's first-hand observations. "Admittedly, contractor performance was uneven and Iranian forces continued to suffer from command and logistical problems ..."[35]

Iran, despite its US-friendly Shah, went along with its fellow Saudi Arabia-led OPEC members — at least in rhetoric. In 1973, Iran was second only behind Saudi Arabia in output.[36] It shortly decided not to go along with the rest of its OPEC neighbors, which only fueled Irans' already restive and rising nationalistic internal political situation, and raised the eyebrows of the West. Beginning in 1974, OPEC gradually relaxed its grip in fear of wrecking Western economies that they themselves also were dependent upon.

The spring of 1977 saw a destabilization of revenue for Iran because of Saudi Arabia's flood of crude oil after the

---

[35] Rubin, Barry, *Paved With Good Intentions: The American Experience and Iran.* Oxford University Press, 1980.

[36] Seymour, Ian. *OPEC Instrument of Change.* Saint Martin's Press, 1981.

1973 embargo and the aftermath — undermining the rest of the OPEC nations. Iran tried to compete with the Saudi's because of their own falling revenues, but held the price-line. "The Americans had finally lost patience with their Iranian ally, whose aggressive oil policies threatened not only Iran's economy but also the economies of Western allies in Europe and Asia. The U.S.-Saudi gambit worked and oil prices stayed in line."[37] To undermine and punitively punish the unsteady ally, newly minted President Carter openly called for an arms embargo against the Shah for human rights violations.

The consequences for Iran was devastating for its ability to pay for a military build-up and internal stability. Many Iranian's were put out of work, similar to what happened to the 1974 US economy. Despite the lavish military and construction projects, now drying up, the Iranian government was outlaying nearly two-thirds of its budget to social welfare programs.[38] Despite the expenditures, the Shah's White Revolution of modernization was quickly coming to an end. In a strange way, it was a victim of its own success: it strengthened the rising middle class (the bourgeois) merchants and students, and the theocratic classes, who were pushing in different directions, but always against the aristocrat royal family. The Shah's intended audience was to win over the working and peasant classes, however, they too pushed back and generally ended up in the theocratic pew. It was the repeat of the 18th century French Revolution Estates-General: the clergy, the nobility, and the rest. Despite complaints of religious impurities caused by The

---

[37] Cooper, Andrew Scott. *The Fall of Heaven: The Pahlavis and the Final Days of Imperial Iran.* New York: Henry Holt and Company, 2016, page 231.

[38] US State Department, Country Reports on Human Rights Practices, (Washington, 1978).

White Revolution, the theocratic class of Iran certainly had a grievance with the Shah who sought land reform of which they are large holders.

The 1973 Yom Kippur War was really the last straw, and an affirmation for OPEC nations to move against the US, who also reacted to Nixon's sea-changing unilateral decision to remove the US from the Gold Standard in 1971. The result was in a drop in the value of the dollar, hurting OPEC countries in their revenue exchange. Nixon's actions effectively ended the World War II era Bretton Woods agreement. Nixon and capital interests removed themselves from the Gold Standard in-short because the drain of gold going to other countries (OPEC nations, for example, typically wanted payment in gold, not paper).

Cold War Nixon policy was not concerned with OPEC turning to the Soviet Union — the OPEC nations viewed them with equal suspicion and as a competitor. The OPEC nations had turned themselves into a *de facto* united states of OPEC. A unity of nations as a direct threat to US national oil security. Oil became the real weapon for the Middle-East centric OPEC nations to use against US policies.

"In addition to King Faisal's concerns regarding the US policy toward the Arab-Israeli conflict, he was frustrated when the US supplied Iran with its most sophisticated weaponry in an effort to replace the British presence in the Persian Gulf. The US had been withholding such types of sophisticated equipment from those Arab countries that needed and asked for them."[39] The West was re-affirming favor with another nation in the Middle East: non-Arab Iran, an ancient and modern nemesis of Saudi Arabia and Iraq.

In WWII, Iran was coveted for its oil and strategic location: just south of the Allied USSR, west of the British protectorates and to the South the neighboring more oil-rich nations like Saudi Arabia.

The pre-war German government had long attempted to lure Iran into their sphere of influence, and the wily Shah played many sides. British oil companies already had a foothold on the Iranian south fields. With the threat from Nazi Germany, the British government and oil companies made sure they held onto them tenaciously.

Complicating the theatre was the USSR, an Allied member acting more as an old Imperial power exerting its influence into northern Iran, competing with Britain imperial interests. The Allies were worried about the Shah's clumsy flirtations with the Nazi government. The British and Russians were resented by the Shah as imperial powers attempting to dominate Iran. In Operation Countenance in 1941, Britain and the Soviet Union invaded and promptly disposed of the Shah, and placed his son, Mohammad Reza Pahlavi, as the new Shah, (the Shah of the same era as this book subject) who reigned until his disposal in the Revolution of 1979.

Enter the Americans into the region. At first, the pre-war Americans were viewed more favorably by the Shah

---

[39] *Oil & Gas Journal*: The 1973 oil embargo: its history, motives, and consequences. May 2005. http://www.ogj.com/articles/print/volume-103/issue-17/general-interest/the-1973-oil-embargo-its-history-motives-and-consequences.html [citing F. Itayim, "Arab Oil-The Political Dimension," *Journal of Palestine Studies* 3, Winter 1974: 84-97.

because of US isolationist and non-interventionist views at the time. The American oil companies, already operating in Saudi Arabia, eyed the Iran fields and were lukewarmly invited by the Shah as early as 1941. The forced love triangle between the Big Three presented a predicament for the Americans who were allied with both *de facto* powers already in the region. But, hey, why not invite oneself into the party of friends! The Shah was more accepting of the Americans, who had pretended criticisms of imperial Britain and Russia and other colonial powers.

Inevitably, the world war caused the Allies Britain and Russia to intervene in Iran for strategic reasons preventing the Axis powers from obtaining a foothold. German General Erwin Rommel's North African push to the oil-rich east failed by 1943 and put the Nazi's effectively out of range geographically and politically.

Not to be outmaneuvered, the Americans arrived with their first troops in 1943. The British could only look the other way and trust. The Russians didn't trust but acquiesced because those troops opened up a corridor of supplies to them from the USA in continuing their war effort against the Axis. To bless the Allied domination over Iran, and with the polite invitation of the Shah, the Tehran Conference met publicly in November 1943, to confer about the future of Europe and colonial territories after the war.

Toward the close of the war, Russian actions in the region seemed more old Czarist imperialism mixed with southern border security concerns rather than ideology. The USSR was not as bold with Iran as it was in Eastern Europe and the coming veil of the "Iron Curtin". Why so tepid with Iran? Northern Iran didn't have the oil reserves like its south; the USSR was multi-occupied with consolidating power in Eastern Europe; resolving its own restive internal satraps; weighing the high political costs of outright intervention up against the British and Americans already having a physical hold; and it was just worn out from a devastating world war. The USSR instead busied itself with support with pro-soviet parties in the Ukraine, the Azerbaijani and the Kurds. The USSR was more concerned with encouraging the somewhat independent and new Tudeh Party of Iran, a Marxist movement with grassroots origins in the north of Iran.

As the Iron Curtin tore the Big Three allies asunder and birthed the Cold War, American oil interests muscled into the market.

The Shah pressed both the Americans and British for oil rights. The Russians fumed but were largely rebuffed by their fair-weather friend the Shah, particularly after the USSR occupied northern parts of Iran during the war (but later withdrew). The Shah was increasingly suspicious of the Russians, out of proximity of geography and the rise of the contumacious Tudeh Party.

The White Revolution of the Shah in post-war WWII was westernization for the purpose of modern militarization for past glory and against its old nemesis Saudi Arabia. The Americans were most happy to supply that training in the early 1950s and along with it some cultural influences. It was this slow infusion of western military and culture that raised the eyebrows of the cultural and religious citizens. It was a coming collide of the western-looking but despotic Shah, and the democratic seeking indigenous populace.

By the early 1950s, the new Cold War was full-blown and the WASP Calvinist views shaped "The West" — those of the Saved and those the predestined Damned. Fear of the

USSR, real, unreal or self-serving, solidified US policy of the saved and unsaved geopolitical camps. Eventually the US "... described the situation in the Near East vis-a-vis the Soviet Union as being that Greece constituted the left flank, Turkey the center, and Iran the right flank."[40] The British Empire was collapsing and wane. Iran now was provisionally in the US church pew of Cold War containment policy.

The 1953 Iranian *coup d'ètat* against parliamentarily elected Prime Minister Mohammad Mosaddegh, congealed the US presence in the Middle East. Not only was Mosaddegh a victim of convenient US Cold War policy, but a victim of hard-luck. Dr. Mosaddegh's real problem was contending with the British controlled oil fields — and getting Iran's rightful share of the sales. US Secretary of State Dean Acheson told Mosaddegh that the US wanted no part in upsetting the international oil community (including the US who was making inroads into Iran). Indeed, the cash-strapped Mosaddegh government came hat-in-hand to sell oil to the USA. Acheson saw what was coming and attempted to deal down the price of oil, arguing a glut on the world market.[41] The stage was set against the Prime Minister.

Mosaddegh's bigger "crime" was his popularity with the Iranian people, his secular, democratic government in a Third World, and his objections to US policies toward Iran.

---

[40] Acheson Papers, Secretary of State File. *Interview between the President and the Shah of Iran, November 18, 1949.*

[41] Acheson Papers, Secretary of State File. *Memorandum of Conversation with Prime Minister Mohammad Mosaddegh of Iran, Assistant Secretary of State George G. McGhee, Paul Nitze and Lieutenant Colonel Walters, October 24, 1951.*

He was branded too Left for the US and it smelled like Moscow influence to Washington. Mosaddegh was a constitutional monarchist, and an anti-socialist and had no part of the Tudeh Party, but that didn't matter to Acheson and company — control needed to be handed back firmly with the malleable Shah. The Prime Minister led the Iranian Parliament to vote for nationalization of the oil companies. It was all over by that act. A nationalized, free-enterprise company would automatically paint the picture Communist through the lens of the 1950s US State Department. Upon nationalization, the British embargoed the nation by 1951 creating more economic woes for the Iranian Prime Minister.

The Iranian National Front (1949-1981) was composed of secular politicians and emerging Islamist leaders. It was an uneasy alliance, but both opposed the Shah and his friendliness with the West. Yet both Mosaddegh and his religious counterpart, Ayatollah Abol-Ghasem Kashani, were anti-socialist. The US State Department was not really interested in the ideological war with International Communism, but rather the oil fields in Iran and some window-dressing notion of Communist containment since Iran bordered with the USSR. Despite the oil glut on the market and the depressed prices, the ideology of preserving the oil companies prevailed. Indeed, "Whatever his faults, Mossadegh had no love for the Russians and timely aid might enable him to keep Communism in check."[42]

Mosaddegh's economic problems became worse with the British embargo. His popularity started to decline and there was widespread disenchantment with his administration. By 1953 he was disposed of by British Secret Service

---

[42] Wilford, Hugh. *America's Great Game: The CIA's Secret Arabists and the Making of the Modern Middle East*. Basic Books, 2013.

and US Central Intelligence Agency operatives. By this time even the religious wing represented by Kashani "supported" the Shah. Mosaddegh's fate was sealed. "For many Iranians, the coup demonstrated duplicity by the United States, which presented itself as a defender of freedom but did not hesitate to use underhanded methods to overthrow a democratically elected government to suit its own economic and strategic interests", the Agence France-Presse reported.[43]

Thus, the 1953 coup debacle was the first open wound between the USA and Iran. The second was the embassy hostage taking in 1979. As the old cliché says, "Two wrongs do not make a right."

I was shocked in 1979, having visited Iran only two years before, to see a theocracy movement the force behind the revolution. I wasn't the only one shocked, as historians have been deliberating that history ever since.

As Dr. Andrew Scott Cooper at the Ford Museum succinctly put, Iranians are the "most pro-American in the region with the most anti-American government."[44] By 1978, 52,000[45] Americans resided in Iran and had the largest American ex-patriate community in the world. So why the so-called clash of cultures? The succinct answer is that Iran

---

[43] ABS • CBN News, Sgt. E. A. Esguerra Avenue, Quezon City, Philippines, https://news.abs-cbn.com/world/06/04/09/obama-admits-us-involvement-1953-iran-coup

[44] Cooper, Andrew Scott. "The US, Iran, and the Fall of the Shah"; May 16, 2017 lecture; https://geraldrfordfoundation.org/andrew-scott-cooper-us-iran-fall-shah/

[45] Cooper, Andrew Scott. *The Fall of Heaven: The Pahlavis and the Final Days of Imperial Iran.* New York: Henry Holt and Company, 2016.

has always been a link between Western and Eastern commerce since Alexander the Great (and probably earlier). It has enjoyed both worlds. Although introduced to what we call Iran today in 640 C.E., Islam played a powerful part but was largely tolerant of other religions and foreigners traversing its territories. It grew in science and culture while grappling with its Sunni and Shia religious divisions and the intrigues from its neighbors.

In 1979, The US-led powers still held to the old Cold War policies of containment against the USSR. The USSR interest in the Iranian Revolution of 1979 was tepid: it viewed it with conflicting anxiety — a restive Islamic movement on its border and the Iranian clergy were no friends of the atheist Soviets. Indeed, after the dust settled with the American Embassy Hostage crisis, the Iranian government became hostile critics of the USSR: its invasion of Afghanistan and its muted support of the Iranian Tudeh Party. The USSR welcomed the Revolution only because it upset the power relationship with the US in the region — it became a cheer-leader only.[46]

Regardless, a revolution against an established friend of the US was considered knee-jerk anti-American without considering, perhaps, revolutions do happened for other reasons.

The rising secular pro-European parliamentarian politicians, such as Seyyed Abolhassan Banisadr, were branded too left for the Cold Warriors. Consequently, support for the only democratic forces rising out of the Revolution were suffocated by neglect from the West and the vacuum was filled by the theocratic right wing. By late 1979 the Ayatol-

---

[46] Intelligence Memorandum, Central Intelligence Agency, 14 December 1979; Subject: IRAN: Relations with the USSR; Top Secret (approved for release 23 November 2005).

SHAHBAZ 77

lah Sayyid Ruhollah Mūsavi Khomeini had solidified the Revolution in his persona of the French First Estate (clergy). He quickly kicked out the Second Estate (the nobility) which had been at odds with each other since the 1920s. He embraced the uneasy allied Third Estate (the rest) which has been since systemically repressed, seeded some window-dressing of democracy.

§ § §

So why was Exercise Shahbaz 77 so important? Was it just a training exercise?

Iran had a large standing army. It's air force, "... received the highest priority, in terms of the allocation of money and manpower, as it was perceived by the Shah as the most important element of deterrence, and as a vehicle for using Iranian power against a long-range target" — probably it's nemeses Iraq and Saudi Arabia.[47] The Shah long desired a return to the glory of Persia past, and as long as he bought arms from the USA and allies, so the USA was happy.

1) *It was a Training Mission.* Interoperability between the USA and other friendly nations occurred all the time. Col. McInerney, in the exercise newsletter, so stated the mission of Exercise Shahbaz 77.

2) The USA was *sending a rapid deployment message* to the Shah. Rapid Deployment Force was a "new" concept and Shahbaz 77 was probably the first — at least our food service unit was the first. First in the sense of cobbling together other diverse units from various parts of the far-flung American defense forces to a desired location. For our food service unit, we were truly cobbled together as all

---

[47] Tan, Andrew T. H. *The Global Arms Trade: A Handbook.* New York: Routledge, 2010.

SHAHBAZ 77

members came from various parts of USAFE and were put to work together. Instead of an entire food service organization from one particular base deployed, we came out of many units. The other units in Shahbaz 77 kept their cohesion, squadrons, and wings together and never were mated with other members.

Part (3a) would help the Shah with any internal or external enemies. It demonstrated the USA could deploy rapidly to his rescue or extract people and material quickly if needed.

Part (3b) would let the Shah know the USA could, at will, intervene in Iran if the Shah changed allegiance or was disposed of. Personally, knowing the size of the Imperial forces, logistics and unforgiving terrain of the country, that would have been wishful thinking.

4) Shahbaz 77 *lit the match of the revolution.* Okay, that's a big and probably controversial statement. Despite a large American population in Iran in 1977 and a small military contingent in Tehran and elsewhere, Shabhaz 77 was the first, albeit small, military exercise into Iran with the purpose other than weapons training and sales. The USA was training for intervention in my analysis. Yes, other NATO countries had trained with the Iranian armed forces, but they were mostly in conjunction with arms sales.

The resentment of foreign forces of even a small magnitude was enough to stoke the fire of discontent. This foreign policy mistake was repeated with the USA quartering troops in Saudi Arabia in 1990 and lead to the rise of indignant men like Osama bin-Laden.

Without giving credence to a conspiracy… 1977+ was seeing the rise of the Religious Right all around the world. In Iran, the Middle East, and in the USA culminating in the politicized 1980 election of Ronald Reagan with "Moral Majority" Jerry Falwell's help. Restive Catholic Poland birthed Solidarity by 1980, sealed with countryman Karol J. Wojtyla's election as Pope John Paul II and his return to conservative theology. More so, the rise of religious nationalist movements in the Muslim world in the late 1970s and so on, later discombobulated and accelerated by the Iraq War's 1990-1991 and 2003-2011.

Historians argue today about the Iranian revolution and its true meaning. The leaders of the conflict, and there are many sides, may play the pieces of geopolitics, but as the old Persian saying goes "A mountain never meets a mountain, but a man meets a man." An understanding between nations will never be envisaged because it takes that people-to-people connection. I just hope I did a little in Iran.

Bibliography

ABS • CBN News, Sgt. E. A. Esguerra Avenue, Quezon City, Philippines, https://news.abs-cbn.com/world/06/04/09/obama-admits-us-involvement-1953-iran-coup

Acheson Papers, Secretary of State File. *Memorandum of Conversation with Prime Minister Mohammad Mosaddegh of Iran, Assistant Secretary of State George G. McGhee, Paul Nitze and Lieutenant Colonel Walters, October 24, 1951.*

Acheson Papers, Secretary of State File. *Interview between the President and the Shah of Iran, November 18, 1949.*

[AI] *Amnesty International Report 1 June 1975-31 May 1976.* London: Amnesty International Publications, 1976.

Central Intelligence Agency, Intelligence Memorandum, 14 December 1979; Subject: IRAN: Relations with the USSR; Top Secret (approved for release 23 November 2005).

Cooper, Andrew Scott. *The Fall of Heaven: The Pahlavis and the Final Days of Imperial Iran.* New York: Henry Holt and Company, 2016.

Cooper, Andrew Scott. *The US, Iran and the Fall of the Shah,* May 16, 2017, Ford Museum, Grand Rapids, Michigan, Youtube video.

Dimkrakis, Panagiotis. *Failed Alliances of the Cold War: Britain's Strategy and Ambitions in Asia and the Middle East.* New York: Tauris Academic Studies, 2011.

IRIS, document 1020185 Wing/Military Airlift Command Operations, (unclassified); document 01030293 United States Logistics Group (classified), US Air Force history index. Released in 1985.

Isenberg, David. *Cato Institute Policy Analysis No. 44: The Rapid Deployment Force: The Few, The Futile, the Expendable.* Cato Institute, 1984.

Mann, James. *Rise of the Vulcans: The History of Bush's War Cabinet.* Penguin Book, 2004.

Oil & Gas Journal: The 1973 oil embargo: its history, motives, and consequences. May 2005. http://www.ogj.com/articles/print/volume-103/issue-17/general-interest/the-1973-oil-embargo-its-history-motives-and-consequences.html [citing F. Itayim, "Arab Oil-The Political Dimension," *Journal of Palestine Studies* 3, Winter 1974: 84-97.

Rubin, Barry, *Paved With Good Intentions: The American Experience and Iran.* Oxford University Press, 1980.

Tan, Andrew T. H. *The Global Arms Trade: A Handbook.* New York: Routledge, 2010.

Seymour, Ian. *OPEC Instrument of Change.* Saint Martin's Press, 1981.

United States Air Force, *Shahbaz 77: A Newsletter For USAF Personnel Deployed to Shiraz AFB Iran.* April 1977. [NXL]

US House of Representatives, Subcommittee on Evaluation, Permanent Select Committee on Intelligence, Staff Report. *Iran: Evaluation of U.S. Intelligence Performance Prior to November 1978* (Washington DC: GPO, 1979).

US State Department, Country Reports on Human Rights Practices, (Washington, 1978).

Wilford, Hugh. *America's Great Game: The CIA's Secret Arabists and the Making of the Modern Middle East.* Basic Books, 2013.

SHAHBAZ 77

APPENDIX

KNOWN EXERCISE SHAHBAZ 77 PARTICIPANTS

BELL, Capt. Glenn E. Weapons system officer, 52nd TFW, from South Carolina. (*The Gaffney Ledger*, South Carolina, May 9, 1977, page 7).
BISHOP, SSgt. Marty. Food Service Specialist.
BLACK, Capt. Don 52nd TFW. [NXL]
BUHROW, Col. Robert E., Commander, 52nd TFW. Retired in 1982 as a Brigadier General, assistant deputy director of deployment operations, Joint Deployment Agency at MacDill Air Force Base, Florida. A veteran of the Vietnam War, he was awarded the Distinguished Flying Cross. [USAF]
CHAMBERLAIN, MSgt. Douglas. Food Service Specialist.
CLARK, Capt. Jack, II from Fayetteville, Arkansas (*Northwest Arkansas Times,* Fayetteville, Arkansas, June 5, 1977, page 22).
CLEPPER, SrA. Michael W. Baytown, Texas (*The Baytown Sun*, Baytown, Texas, May 23, 1977, page 9).
COOK, SSgt. John. Food Service Specialist.
CRONIN, SrA. William Weapons Control Systems specialists from Seymour, Connecticut, with the 52nd TFW, (*Naugatuck Daily News*, Naugatuck, Connecticut, May 11, 1977, page 5).
DAVIS, Sgt. Chris 52nd TFW. [NXL]
DAVIS, Capt. Richard S., Jr. Lumberton, North Carolina, 401st TFW, (*The Robesonian*, Lumberton, North Carolina, May 31, 1977, page 6).
DUVALL, Tsgt. George E. Aerospace ground equipment technician, 20th TFW, from West Virginia. (*Alamogordo Daily News*, Alamogordo, New Mexico, May 12, 1977, page 22).
EALOWSKE, Msgt. Thomas Finance agent. [NXL]
ELLIS, A1C Robert. Food Service Specialist.
GOLDEN, Capt. (Dr.) John Graham. Veterinarian, 50th Tactical Hospital, from Texas. Colonel (Dr.) John Graham Golden, USAF (Ret.), died unexpectedly June 26, 2010 in San Antonio. Entered military service in 1970 as a member of the United States Air Force Veterinary Corps. He was the last active duty research veterinarian in the Air Force prior to the Air Force Veterinary Corps being abolished in 1981. Golden's last active duty assignment from 1988 until his retirement was as Director of the Veterinary Sciences Department for the USAF School of Aerospace Medicine, Brooks Air Force Base (AFB), San Antonio. Other assignments during his career included the Air Force Institute of Technology with assignment at the Hershey Medical Center, Pennsylvania. Golden received numerous military decorations as well as the 1994 Outstanding Alumnus Award for Government Research from Texas A&M University College of Veterinary Medicine. (obituary, San Antonio Texas, *Express-News,* June 28, 2010).

SHAHBAZ 77

HALL, Lt. Col. Henry V. Commander, 23rd TFS. [NXL]

HOOPER, A1C. Curtis L. Weapons Mechanic, 20th TFW, from Maryland, (*The Daily Times*, Salisbury, Maryland, June 4, 1977, page 3).

JAMES, Lt. Col. William K. 55th TFS commander. Major General James was director of the Defense Mapping Agency, Fairfax, Va., 1990-1993.

General James was born in Hope, Ark.

James served with the 3rd Tactical Fighter Wing, Bien Hoa Air Base, Republic of Vietnam, in February 1969. During this tour of duty he flew 180 combat missions. In December 1975 General James became commander of the 55th Tactical Fighter Squadron, 20th Tactical Fighter Wing, at Royal Air Force Station Upper Heyford, England. He had many other assignments. His military awards and decorations include the Distinguished Service Medal, Legion of Merit, Distinguished Flying Cross, Meritorious Service Medal, Air Medal with eight oak leaf clusters, Air Force Commendation Medal, Republic of Vietnam Campaign Medal, and Armed Forces Expeditionary Medal. He retired July 1, 1993. [USAF].

LOOY, 1st Lt. Neil M. Aircraft commander, 52nd TFW, from California, (*Valley News*, Van Nuys, California, June 1, 1977, page 16).

LOUGEE, A1C. Thomas P. Telecommunications Operations Specialist, 1st Combat Communications Squadron, from Chambersburg, Pennsylvania.

MCINERNEY, Col. Thomas G. Commander of Exercise Shahbaz 77, from 20th TFW. General McInerney was born in Havre de Grace, Md.

He took part in the Berlin and Cuban crises in 1962, flying escort missions in the Berlin Corridor and escort reconnaissance missions over Cuba. In April 1963 he was one of the first forward air controllers assigned to South Vietnam with a Vietnamese army division.

In August 1974 he became the air attache to the U.S. Embassy in London. There he worked for three different ambassadors, assisting them in changing U.S. policy toward the multi-role combat aircraft, and increased standardization with European aerospace and North Atlantic Treaty Organization air forces.

From November 1976 until October 1977 he was vice commander of the 20th Tactical Fighter Wing, Royal Air Force Station Upper Heyford, England. He had many other assignments.

His military awards and decorations include the Distinguished Service Medal, Defense Superior Service Medal, Legion of Merit with oak leaf cluster, Distinguished Flying Cross with oak leaf cluster, Bronze Star Medal with "V" device and oak leaf cluster, Meritorious Service Medal with oak leaf cluster, Air Medal with 17 oak leaf clusters, Air Force Commendation Medal with oak leaf cluster and Vietnam Service Medal with six service stars. He has also been awarded the Third Order of the Rising Sun by the Japanese government.

In addition, the general was inducted into the Order of the Sword in July 1980. This award recognizes both military and civilian individuals for conspicuous and significant contributions to the welfare and prestige of the noncommissioned officer corps and the military establishment. The general was the sixth Pacific Air Forces officer and the 63rd officer overall inducted into the order since the Air Force became a separate branch of the armed services in 1947.

He was promoted to lieutenant general Oct. 8, 1986, with same date of rank. He retired July 1, 1994. Lieutenant General Thomas G. McInerney was assistant vice chief of staff, Headquarters U.S. Air Force, Washington, D.C. He is responsible for the organization and administration of the Air Staff.

General McInerney was also a well known Fox News television personality. An early "birther", in 2010 he supported Terrence Lakin who refused to deploy to Afghanistan because he believed President Obama was not a legitimate president. In 2014 he postulated the theory that Malaysia Airlines Flight 370 was hijacked to Pakistan for terrorist reasons. In 2017, on Fox's Sean Hannity show, he dismissed the millions who would died on the Korean peninsula in event of a nuclear war.

He is also author with Paul E. Vallely, *Endgame: The Blueprint for Victory in the War on Terror, 2004*. Member of the Iran Policy Committee, 2005. Fox News "The O'Reilly Factor," 2006. In 2014 McInerney suggested "We've got Muslim Brotherhood in the U.S. government today." Pressed to elaborate on the allegation, McInerney added, "I haven't got their names exactly but there's a list of them, at least 10 or 15 of them in the U.S. government."

In May 2018 he made news again by calling Senator John McCain "Songbird McCain" because of McCain's imprisonment in Hanoi during the Vietnam War. [USAF and various other sources]

MOORE, Msgt. Billy C. Integrated Avionics systems supervisor, 20th TFW, from Texas, (*The Waxahachie Daily Light*, Waxahachie, Texas, May 22, 1977, page 8).

MOORE, Sgt. Glen H. Telecommunications Operations Specialist, 1st Combat Communications Squadron. [NXL]

POTTER, A1C Paula. Food Service Specialist.

REUBEN, A1C. Derek A. Food Service Specialist, 48th Combat Support Group, from Philadelphia, Pennsylvania. [USAF]

SANDERS, A1C. Curtis "Curt" D. Food Service Specialist, 48th Combat Support Group, from Mercersburg, but born in Chambersburg, Pennsylvania. He enlisted into the USAF in March 1975 after working as a printing press operator. After his duty at RAF Lakenheath, he was posted to Malmstrom AFB, Great Falls, Montana, 341st Services Squadron, Strategic Air Command. Promoted to Senior Airman, Sergeant and Staff Sergeant. Upon Honorable discharge in 1980, he attended Harrisburg Area Community College, 1980-1982, earning an Associate of Arts, Liberal Arts, and then Pennsylvania State University, Middletown, 1982-1984, graduating with a Bachelor of Social Science, major in Public Policy. He had various professions upon graduation mostly in office management, finally retiring after 20 years with the Commonwealth of Pennsylvania in 2015 as Data Management Analyst in the Office of the Budget. [USAF; author]

SCHELL, Maj. John F. (*The Post-Standard,* Syracuse, New York, May 13, 1977, page 15).

SHARPE Jr., Capt. Ervin C. "Sandy" Operations officer, 52nd TFW, (*The Daily Standard,* Sikeston, Missouri, June 14, 1977, page 12).: Major General Sandy Sharpe was director of operations, Headquarters Air Combat Command, Langley Air Force Base, Va. July 1974 - August 1977, flight commander, 23rd Tactical Fighter Squadron, Spangdahlem Air Base, West Germany; and many other assignments. Awards: Defense Superior Service Medal, Legion of Merit with oak leaf cluster, Distinguished Flying Cross, Meritorious Service Medal with oak leaf cluster, Air Medal with 15 oak leaf clusters, Air Force Commendation Medal with oak leaf cluster. Retired September 1, 1998. [USAF]

SMARTZ, SSgt. James. Food Service Specialist.

SMITH, A1C. James T. Computer operator, Incirlik Common Defense Installation, Turkey, from Texas, (*The Port Arthur News*, Port Arthur, Texas, July 4, 1977, page 5).

SPEARS, Sgt. Drew E. Jet engine mechanic, 52nd TFW, from Texas, (*The La Marque Times*, June 15, 1977, page 17).

STEVENS, A1C Mark. Food Service Specialist.

STORMS, SSgt. Tony. Food Service Specialist.

THOMAS, A1C. Mark L. Food Service Specialist, 48th Combat Support Group. [USAF]

THORPE, Msgt. Thomas 435th TAW. [NXL]

STRANATHAN, A1C. Robert W. From Colorado (*Gazette-Telegraph*, Colorado Springs, Colorado, May 15, 1977, page 35.)

ULREY, A1C. John From Ohio, (*The Daily Reporter*, Dover, Ohio, June 30, 1977, page 26).

WESTRA, Lt. Col. (Dr.) John P. Commander, Air Transportable Hospital, 50th TFW. Born in 1941 in Little Falls, New York, Dr. Westra died November 25, 1980 of illness in Pensacola, Florida. He had a family practice in San Bernardino, California for ten years, then the last 18 months of his life as the assistant director of residency program in family practice, Eglin AFB, Florida. (obituary, *Argus-Leader*, Sioux Falls, South Dakota, November 26, 1980, page 17.)

WHITTAKER, SSgt. Carl R. Aircraft pneudraulic [sic] systems technician, 52nd TFW, from Wisconsin, (*Stevens Point Journal*, Stevens Point, Wisconsin, May 18, 1977, page 8).

WITTE, Sgt. Kerry D. Inventory Management Specialist, 1st Combat Squadron, from Missouri, (*Mexico Ledger*, Mexico, Missouri, July 20, 1977, page 9).

YOST, Sgt. Lee Ann. Food Service Specialist, 20th Combat Support Group. [NXL]

SHAHBAZ 77

KNOWN UNITS IN EXERCISE SHAHBAZ 77

1st Combat Communications Squadron, Lindsey Air Station, Germany.
8th Aerial Port Squadron, RAF Mildenhall, England.
20th Combat Support Group, RAF Upper Heyford, England.
20th Tactical Fighter Wing, RAF Upper Heyford, England.
23rd Tactical Fighter Squadron, Spangdahlem, Germany.
48th Combat Support Group, RAF Lakenheath, England.
50th Tactical Hospital, Hahn AB, Germany.
52nd Tactical Fighter Wing, Spangdahlem, Germany.
55th Tactical Fighter Squadron, RAF Upper Heyford, England.
62nd Military Airlift Wing.
401st Tactical Fighter Wing, Torrejon de Ardoz, Spain.
435th Military Airlift Command Control Element, Rhein-Main AB, Germany.
513th Tactical Airlift Wing, RAF Mildenhall, England.
Carrier Airborne Early Warning Squadron VAW-125.
Incirlik Common Defense Installation, Turkey.
Shiraz Air Force Base, Shiraz, Iran.
USS John F. Kennedy.

The author, Curt Sanders, at Persepolis, Iran, April 1977.

DEPARTMENT OF THE AIR FORCE
HEADQUARTERS 48TH COMBAT SUPPORT GROUP (USAFE)
APO NEW YORK 09179

CENTO TRAVEL ORDER

Country of Origin THE UNITED STATES OF AMERICA   Order Number TA-438

1. The bearer, A1C CURTIS D. SANDERS, ███████████, will travel from RAF Lakenheath, England to Shiraz AB, Iran via USAF Military Aircraft/Commercial Aircraft, on or about 7 Apr 77. Expected date of return is 6 May 77.
2. Authority is not granted to possess and carry arms.
3. The person named in paragraph 1 is authorized to carry NO sealed dispatches, containing only official documents, numbered N/A .
4. I hereby certify that this individual is a member of a force as defined in the CENTO Status of Forces Agreement, and that this is an authorized move under the terms of this agreement.

GEORGE SM. PENNE, SMSgt, USAF
Ass"t Chief, Central Base Administration

www.ingramcontent.com/pod-product-compliance
Lightning Source LLC
Chambersburg PA
CBHW031413040426
42444CB00005B/548